ROAD TO 99

WRITE. RECORD. REFLECT. REPEAT

JEREMY SCHREIFELS

Road to 99

Write. Record. Reflect. Repeat.

ISBN: 978-1-946694-63-8

Edited by: Hilary Jastram & David Rynne

Cover Design by: Empty Page Studios

Author photo credit: Erica Ann Photography

Publisher: Bookmark Publishing

WHERE THE ROAD BEGAN...

"A lot of you are shitting on 2020, but in reality, it's the year that made you reflect, increased your self-awareness, maybe it exposed you to new opportunities. It's the year that woke you up... and that will lead to your ultimate happiness. You just don't know it yet."

—Gary Vee

A SONGWRITER

Songwriter: A person who shows up consistently to write songs with others or on their own, records them in some fashion, and then releases them for the world to hear.

—Jeremy Schreifels

TESTIMONIALS

Anthony Sylvers: Videographer and Cinematographer

Not only did Jeremy teach me the fundamentals of music theory, I believe most importantly he was an example of the correct mindset needed to succeed. His passion and drive are inspiring, and he is an example of "you reap what you sow." Hard work pays off, and he instilled that greatly in us.

He taught us to push through the pain. If it hurts, keep going. If it's hard, push through it. Greatness is never easy. Specifically, at the time this was through musical repetition, practice, drill, and memorization, but it can apply to absolutely anything.

You get what you put in, for better or for worse. Do you want it, or not? YOU have to make that decision. I am so thankful that he was my instructor for so many years and this was instilled in my conscience at such a young age.

Matt Wagner: Senior Vice President Sales, Fields Manufacturing

I worked with Jeremy for about four years teaching music. Some say the best way to learn is to teach, and I can certainly say that during my teaching years alongside Jeremy I learned so much that is still relevant and utilized in many aspects of life. But none more applicable than determination.

Learning, teaching, and performing music requires high levels of determination to exercise and execute your craft as an art. That drive is what led to success in my career in business but more importantly, determination taught me how to overcome the many obstacles life throws at you and still keep your head up.

I remember Jeremy once told our students, myself included, that if you make a mistake, don't stop, just keep playing and leave the mistake behind you. Those are words of determination.

Jaymi Struthers: Songwriter, Keyboardist & Mom

When I first started working with Jeremy, he was my instructor for drumline. I was fortunate enough to have worked with him again several years later when we played in a traveling band together. There are many things that I learned from him in those early years that I still put to use today in my everyday life as well as in music.

The main thing that I learned from him was to experience and to love music on a whole new level, rather than just listening to or playing it. I learned to put my whole being into expressing what the music was portraying or expressing myself through music I've written. Through this, I realized my passion for creating something to help move people and communicate without words, and I found myself.

Of course, I've learned a lot of other smaller things too. To be on time is to be late. Being early is being on time. You can do anything that you put your mind to, you just have to be disciplined enough to make it happen. With that, you're only holding yourself back by making excuses. Do the work, and you'll reap what you sow. These are just a few of them.

The biggest thing about learning all these things is that Jeremy didn't just preach them, he lived them. He was a great example in that way and continues to be. He has pushed me past the limits I thought I had and helped shape me into the person I am today. Working with him has been a pleasure and an honor. Even though I probably didn't always like what he pushed me to do at the time, I'm grateful to have worked with someone who believed in me enough to make me believe in myself too! He gave me the tools to build myself as a musician and helped me exercise them. He also helped light the fire to keep me pursuing my dreams and never give up on them.

Colleen C. Orne, Executive Director, Milestones

Over the months of coaching with Jeremy, I was better able to identify personal and professional goals and priorities and, subsequently, act on those goals.

Jeremy created a safe and welcoming space for dialogue and exploration that came with both ease and purpose. His genuineness and desire for those in his midst to succeed (as well as achieve greater peace of mind and body) is evident and unwavering when working with him. While our focus was work and professional growth, his insights and "nudging" encouragement certainly impacted my work/life balance in immeasurable ways.

In short, Jeremy helped me further develop my leadership potential, overcome some longstanding workplace challenges, and most importantly, learn to value myself and define a path forward into the future. I strongly recommend Jeremy to anyone who is considering working with a coach. He is approachable, flexible, patient and encouraging.

Mike Thorseth: Drill Writer, Visual Designer, Adjudicator

I've known Jeremy a long time and a few lessons have stayed with me on the stage, at home in my family life, or just making music with my friends. The most universal lesson that I've learned was the hardest lesson. I'd worked very hard on a piece of marimba music while taking lessons and I thought I'd done a pretty good job. Jeremy listened patiently and when I finished, he quietly asked me to "play it again with feeling." At the time it was incredibly frustrating, but it laid in the framework for the most important lesson I've learned. "Play music [with] feeling." This lesson is the lesson I struggle with the most. It's so easy to get lost in the mechanics of music that I forget that making music is the goal.

The next lesson I learned from Jeremy was learned on the many late nights carpooling home from rehearsals. "Listen." It was such a simple lesson, but such an important one. The transition from making music with a conductor guiding the journey through my eyes to being guided through the ears on stage was an important change. I've always been a good listener to try and match other players or sections as a matter of instinct but being on the stage with a handful of people and locking in took listening to another level. When it locked in, it was amazing. The kick drum and the bass in unison. Hearing "I couldn't tell the kick and bass apart" from the front-of-house mixer was a source of pride grounded in good listening. This lesson applies not just to the stage, but life at home as well. Listen.

Jeremy has always been a teacher. In music and in life. He's challenged me to work harder when my performance wasn't up to par, and he's challenged me to take it easy when it was time to rest.

He's taught me that being better every day in some way was a success, even if it was small. Don't shy away from the hard work because it's most rewarding...and we had some fun along the way.

Brendan Ruane: Grammy Nominated Mix Engineer

When I first met Jeremy, we ended up co-writing a song together smack in the middle of the pandemic. I had never written a song with somebody who wasn't in the same room as me, and I was amazed at how naturally remote songwriting came to him. I would record a simple guitar part and within a few hours, he'd turn that into a complete musical idea. I ended up mixing that project, and luckily it turns out we work pretty well together.

So a few months later I got a call from Jeremy and he said he had a project he was working on with a friend of his and he wanted me to mix it. So I jumped on a Zoom call with Jeremy and Nate and we discussed a few of the details, and got to know each other. When the song files finally showed up, I was expecting something that sounded similar to the song Jeremy and I had worked on a few months prior. I was amazed to find out that it sounded nothing like that song. I quickly learned that this was Jeremy's thing. He's a songwriting chameleon in that he seems to just adapt to whatever style you throw at him, and write/play it with every bit of authenticity that you would expect from somebody who only focuses on that specific genre.

I don't know what the secret is to reaching that level of musicianship. Maybe it's Jeremy's coffee-fueled work ethic and artistic vision. Maybe it's Nate's songwriting abilities and lyrical prowess. Maybe it's the top notch team of studio musicians and engineers Jeremy put together. Maybe it's magic. Maybe it's all of the above. I just know that when you put this group of people together, some pretty incredible music ends up happening.

RESOURCES

The Book
www.RoadTo99Book.com

Let's Write
www.JeremySchreifels.com

Inner Workings of Jeremy Playlist
spoti.fi/3JAbSDH

Empty Page Studios
www.EmptyPageStudios.com

Producer Blend Coffee
www.ArtisanJCoffee.com

The Dumpsterfire
thedumpsterfire.phonesites.com

My Corner Retreat
www.MyCornerRetreat.com

ULTRA-MEGA Band
www.UltraMegaBand.com

Mark Stone and the Dirty Country Band
www.LagrungeMusic.com

TABLE OF CONTENTS

FOREWORD

"Don't die with the music still in you."
-Dr. Wayne Dyer

As a bestselling author, speaker, leadership mentor, and coach, I work with entrepreneurs and executives who are extremely successful externally yet are still craving greater fulfillment and impact. They can feel a wealth of untapped power and potential calling them to step into a higher purpose and legacy, knowing they're capable of more. Despite all the success, they're falling short of the freedom and fulfillment, elevated focus and productivity, and financial abundance they're capable of having, which fuels their self-doubt and sabotage cycles. These are the people I wrote my bestselling book, *Be a Boss & Fire That Bitch: Quiet Your Inner Critic & Finally Believe You're GOOD ENOUGH*, for and the people I surround myself with daily in the InFLOWential Leadership Mastermind.

With over 20 years of leadership experience, from leading missions on the front lines of Iraq 2003 to a corporate career to starting, building, struggling, failing, and scaling multiple businesses, I've seen all aspects of the leadership spectrum. Each one taught me that leadership and success are inside jobs. Knowing this allows me to empower my clients to tap into effortless success and influential leadership by unlocking their full gifts and potential through the deepest inner work.

However, that's not where I started. My rock bottom moment was only seven years ago at the time of the writing of this foreword when I was leaning into my own journey of unlocking the music (genius) within me (which happens to be guiding others to their truth and genius). I was my first client. Looking back through my life, music was the constant for understanding my emotions. One of the only ways I could instantly cut through the walls and mask of who I SHOULD be was tapping into the soul of who I was in that moment. You see, I'd spent a lifetime ignoring my music and magic.

Music was my therapy and one of the only ways I knew how to cope with what I was feeling and experiencing when I had no toolkit to support me. Especially when it came time to do the work to heal my past trauma and PTSD. Music therapy was a powerful tool in the healing arsenal, which wouldn't have happened if people like you didn't share the music inside that you're called to create. The world NEEDS your music! To heal and feel, to shine and serve, to lead and succeed.

Over the years, I've met thousands of coaches, experts, and "gurus" in the personal and professional development space. Yet, very few actually embodied the energy and practice of what they taught, instead focusing on marketing and sales over real impact and transformation for their clients. However, Jeremy is different, a true servant leader. Having walked this path himself and leading by example, he's helping people like you simplify the process of sharing your genius with the world. Our power comes from our pain! The key is being willing to own that for the purpose of inspiring others to their own greatness, and that's exactly what Jeremy has done.

The most powerful aspect of the book you're about to read is by following the process Jeremy lays out for you, you'll be able to avoid or quickly work through the internal blocks that come up when sharing a piece of your soul creatively. The fear, impostor syndrome, doubt, overwhelm, and inaction that can be triggered with the thought of creating something that is a representation of our truth and genius, let alone sharing it with others, can lead to hiding, avoidance, analysis paralysis, and inaction. He breaks down, step-by-step, the process of not only activating your untapped potential but also stepping into your true passion and purpose. By the end of this book, not only will you have completed songs, but you'll also have confidence in YOU!

Now it's time to lean in and start the process!

Stacy Raske
Bestselling Author, Be a Boss & Fire That Bitch
CEO, InFLOWential Leadership Mastermind
Apex Executive Coach
stacyraske.com

INTRODUCTION

"The beautiful thing about learning is that no one can take it away from you."
—B.B. King

Being an artist, a crafter of music, a creator of sonic ideas, and an externalist of that which has been nurtured inside you is why we are creators, to begin with. Looking deep into our thoughts, our stories, our experiences, and our challenges is what pushes us through and drives us to keep on going.

Your journey as a songwriter and/or creator may be at various stages.

1. You're looking for a reason to start.
2. You've had some experience but get stuck.
3. You've been creating for years and have hit a lull.
4. Maybe you're full force and just need some inspiration.

Regardless of the reason you chose to pick up and begin sifting through these pages, I encourage you to listen to that soft voice inside of you that pushed you here and allow it to speak louder as your journey on the Road to 99 begins.

I had a defining moment in 1994 that changed my life. That summer evening, as I was driving my 1987 Chrysler New Yorker Fifth Avenue down the river road I'd traveled dozens of times, I cranked the wheel toward the river on what we called "Dead man's curve." In a split second, as my tires hit the gravel, my body immediately slammed the brakes. I sat there, on the side of the road, heart racing, blood pumping, just listening.

Music saved my life.

The song playing on the radio, the beats, the melodies, the words allowed my foot to be removed from the brake and my hands to steer the car back onto the road and make it the rest of the way home that evening.

The power of that song, which to this day, I am still trying to remember, put me back on the road and saved my life.

While we never know who is going to listen to our songs—how they will choose to listen, or who will share our songs with them—they will never have the opportunity to change, affect, or save someone's life if we never write, record, and release them.

It can certainly seem overwhelming at first. To know and feel like the power of your music can move and change people. Just think about your favorite song, your "pump you up" jam, or a song that sparks a memory of a loved one for a moment.

I bet you named a song for all three of those.

These may not have been "hit songs" or "chart-toppers," but you connected to them in some way. Once I had the opportunity to sift through so many parts of my journey and my Road, a resonating anthem kept playing over and over in my head. *People deserve to hear your music. You have a voice. Share it.*

YOU are the only one like YOU.

Not that I want you to feel a heavy responsibility to create. However, I believe that since you are here reading, you already have some of these notions in your brain, body, and spirit.

LET THEM OUT!!!

Make sure to stake markers along your road, document them, post them, send them to others, and share them in your writing sessions. Ideas come from everywhere. Don't ever discount them. Or the process. Hey! Post them and use the hashtag #MYROADTO99!

Once you finish this book, sign and date it. I do this for every book I read. It gives you the opportunity to see what kind of growth you've had since reading the book the last time. Each time you read a book, you are coming away from it with a whole new perspective and so many more experiences to draw from.

My goal is to give you a view to the songwriting process from my 10,000-foot view and experiences. Please note, all the information, experiences, and advice I give throughout is merely based on life and choices made along the way. However, the beauty is, EVERYONE'S journey is unique and provides opportunities no one else will have. Hold onto that.

Enjoy your ride down my Road to 99.

THE ROAD

CHAPTER 1

THE ROAD MAP

"It's not enough to be busy, so are ants.
The question is, 'What are we busy about?'"
-Henry David Thoreau

The Road to 99 doesn't have a road map. It creates a road map. It IS the road map. The hard part to swallow is that it is a never-ending road that appears to be headed in a specific direction and with no apparent destination.

QUESTIONS TO TAKE YOU FURTHER DOWN YOUR PATH

There are a few questions I want you to keep in mind as you discover your Road to 99:

1. What are you trying to achieve?
2. What are you striving for?
3. What defines if you've "made it?"
4. What are you willing to do?
5. What might you sacrifice?
6. Do you have to?
7. Who will come across your path?
8. Who do you want to meet?
9. Will the road you're on be the one you head down?

No, I don't expect you have the answers to all those questions. It's my intention to help you discover them as you journey through these pages.

Begin by taking note of the roads you travel along the way.

What stops are you making?

Are they cities, towns, places you've visited, or maybe they're the people in those spheres?

Take stock of the people who got you there and the new skills you learned.

Follow the web as deep as it goes and keep expanding it. Having these people on your side and in your corner as you continue down the road is essential.

My life mission as a musician and educator has been to just touch one person in the room.

Whether that gets their head bobbing to the kick drum making their heart throb—I call that the "doggy on the dashboard" moment—or they involuntarily start moving and dancing. Many times that becomes my entertainment.

So many times, I have found myself watching a handful of people in the crowd, scanning back and forth, and then there is just that one moment when you start seeing an arm twitch, and a head starts moving ever so slowly up and down. Our bodies "feel" music as such, depending on the decibel levels—and even more when hearing or seeing it.

Or maybe you are like I was in the beginning and didn't even see the heads moving. Your journey to get on your Road to 99 will begin with so many more questions than answers. *Will they think I'm crazy? Will they even take me seriously? Is what I am sharing with them even relevant for them?* Yes, you guessed it, imposter syndrome showed up in my life, as well. I mean, no one is perfect.

It has been at least five years since the beginning of my journey of being a student of songwriting. Notice how I stated that I began with being a "student of." This, at least, establishes that I didn't consider myself a songwriter quite yet. However, I was about to learn and take in as much knowledge as I could.

I read books, took online courses, talked with other songwriters, watched YouTube videos, and listened to thousands of songs across dozens of genres before I even picked up a pen and sat with a notebook.

YES! I said pen and paper. It was a tactile connection between my thoughts, emotions, and stories with the black ink pouring out onto those empty Moleskine pages. The consistent daily practice of putting pen to paper. Thoughts to words and words to statements. Each time, building a new block and making a new connection through burning synapses from my brain to my emotions and releasing those stories.

Songwriters and producers have a continued connection to their songs and what consumers ultimately find emotionally valuable, but many times even more so to the process, the journey, the steps, tactile movements, and the sonic manipulations.

I find that these intricate connections and building blocks of interactions transform the empty page into a life-changing song for the listener. At that point, it becomes a mind, body, and spiritual experience of sonic enjoyment.

It was this "old school" or what the kids these days may call "vintage" that started me down a rabbit hole of daily and weekly writing. Sitting on coffee shop patios, waking up early from a dream, taking just a small moment in the afternoon instead of sneaking in a nap.

I went through two full notebooks before I even started telling people I was writing songs. Until then, I was just writing, or more simply, journaling. Telling stories.

Turning emotional moments into opportunities to put them into words and melodies.

During my high school years, I became intrigued with writing poems. The name of the English teacher who introduced me to poetic writing escapes me. However, I am forever thankful for them.

Whether it was love letters, sonnets, or just short poems about an event or place I traveled to, it was most certainly where the writing truly began. Describing, capturing, painting pictures, and in a very small manner, telling a story. I could've never predicted all those years ago, 25 to be exact, I'd be here typing out this book for you.

In the moment—and at that time—it certainly felt countercultural for being the captain of the drumline. I was supposed to be the "tough drum guy." Not a soft-spoken, gentle writer type.

Since then, I've been fascinated by the writings of Walt Whitman and Edgar Allan Poe. I've even set a few choral works based on poems by Edgar Allan Poe. Poe's work "To The River" spoke so deeply to me that I set the text to music for piano and four vocalists, then had it performed and recorded by a group of performance major students at St. Cloud State University. The lives and choice of words by these poets drove deep into my subconscious and gave me a place to start with creating my lyrics. Let's not forget, this was the first part of my journey.

Now, don't get me wrong—I'm not comparing the level and quality of my songs to that of the writings of some of the world's greatest poets. Merely the discovery of their words, the way they tell stories, and describe people, places, and things provided an entry point for my brain to start putting words together in a story-driven format. With a small amount of education in the literary world from my high school and college classes, I was at a minimum able to understand elements of structure, flow, and unique ways to put them together.

To this day, I continue to read the works of Walt Whitman, Edgar Allan Poe, Jose Medeles, and more. The inner workings and muse of Walt Whitman continue to inspire thought-provoking and overly descriptive ways of describing a time, a place, a scenario, an event, and more. Poets like Whitman have an unprecedented way of delivering a powerful message through words. It seems right to continue to read his words and process what he's saying to enhance and deepen the message and delivery of a lyric.

Edgar Allan Poe has always been intriguing to me. The darkness in his words and muse speak to my inner soul. As you might imagine, since my teenage years were darker moments, Poe's words were like having a conversation with a friend.

So, as I began songwriting as a "verb," something I did as a daily and weekly action, I started with what I knew. Poetry. Not worrying about whether there was even an opportunity to put a melody behind it. Writing about moments in the past, the present, and what the future might be.

BRAIN SHOWERS

In the beginning, I would just begin with a single word as an idea and create *Brain Showers*. Brain Showers is an exercise where you fill an entire sheet of paper starting with one word. That one word leads to the next, each time having the next word be a reaction to the previous word you wrote. At the end of the page, the words you wrote may or may not even pertain to the original word you began with.

In fact, the point is NOT to have them all fit into that one subject or theme. You want your brain to wander and walk on to the next intuitive and immediate word. This exercise—especially the first few times you do it—can feel very uncomfortable.

5/29/17 O.W. "Coffee"

Dark	Roasted	Chilled
Light	brew	Black
nation	iced	fruity
fields	Ground	nutty
bean	sipped	sophisticated
caffeine	aged	Clutch
Espresso	conversation	Cardboard
reserve	dripped	Don't touch
Cream	pour over	Caution
Creme	foamy	be ware
meeting	whipped	Free One
business	short pull	refreshing
mocha	antlers of fur	Status
latte	local	brand
oils	organic	Chatting
Hot	french	laughing
silky smooth	private	complaining
delicatessan	reserve	extra shot
lady of the star	1-pump 2 pump	americano
water	hissing	green
Steamed	grinding	teal
mug	whistling	White
patio	to-go	loud
Sunshine	wind blow	quaint
traffic	honking	tea
chai	frothy	Local Read
Starbucks	Carbon	Liquid Assets
Frothy Monkey		

Sample Brain Shower Exercise from 5/29/2017

These exercises in idea forming, transforming, and development took the poem writing thought process into a more focused and overall "big picture" way of writing. This began what some musicians call a more traditional process of songwriting.

Whatever that really means.

Excuse the sarcasm.

However, as you are about to experience, the process of songwriting is different for everyone.

If there is one thing I have most certainly encountered on this journey, it's that "standard" and "traditional" are just a means of describing a few of the ways it has worked for songwriters and creators in the past. Many of the prescribed methods and thoughts are just someone analyzing thousands of hours of other people's work, sorting them out, and making some semblance of sense.

As songwriters, composers, artists, and creatives in general, we have this tendency to create our blocks. One of the biggest blocks I continue to fight, along with many others, is that of paralysis by analysis. We want to pour over every note, rhythm, lyric, and brushstroke until we perceive each part of the process as "perfect."

IT'S ART, people. There's only the next work of art and the audience's or onlookers' reactions to it.

I attended a songwriting conference one winter, and while conversing with one of the speakers, I asked him why I might struggle so much with writing songs. And by songs, I am referring to the ones you would hear on mainstream radio. After a bit of his investigation through our conversation, he figured out that I was a classically trained composer through my music studies in theory and composition. After which, he let me know that those are some fantastic skills that I brought to the songwriting and creative process. But I should think about using only a few tools at a time. He likened it to a carpenter needing basic tools to get the job done and saving all power and specialty tools for very specific jobs.

Since diving deeper into this process, I find I have more questions... and those questions and vague answers only bring up even more questions. Which I believe is what pushed me down the path and encouraged me to continue learning.

Continue being a student, yes, that's right—a student all over again. Many of the mentors I have chatted with continually refer to this learning mentality as a lifelong opportunity. Not something that you just stop doing once you have left educational institutions.

INSIDER TIP

Set a timer when you do the Brain Shower exercise. Setting a timer, the only boundary around the exercise, puts your brain into the "hot seat," allowing it to perform more efficiently.

CHAPTER 2

THE FOG ON THE ROAD

"The thing that is really hard, and really amazing, is giving up on being perfect and beginning the work of becoming yourself."
—Anna Quindlen

As you are thinking about even more questions, and *how do I just get my songs on the radio for millions to listen to*, you need to clear some of that fog. Create some clarity around the direction you are headed.

The "Hit-Makers" of the songwriting world—though knowing many things that work—are just mindful crafters of avoiding what they know absolutely will not work.

The inner workings of a good song or piece of art are merely putting one's whole self into it and letting the art speak for itself.

Think of each part of your favorite song. One of mine is "Ants Marching" by the Dave Matthews Band. The pure, simple, yet subtle drive to the opening of the song lights a spark that only engulfs you into a raging blue flame by the end of the song with the heightened energy, syncopation, and complex interplay between the band.

After pouring over countless hours of listening, coffee consumption, and dozens of pages of paper, I finally began reaching out to others in search of co-writing and collaboration opportunities. Much to my surprise, I was turned down at every corner.

I think I was only told "no," blown off, and ghosted more times when I was an insurance agent calling prospects.

I was astonished that so many people were unwilling to share in that process. It seemed overwhelmingly crazy to me that other musicians literally weren't interested in collaborating and creating. If we know that we are better in community and collaboration, why are so many just wanting to go alone? Maybe this is a concept for a whole new book!

By that point, in my mind, I was just weeding through all the people who were not yet ready to go on that journey. I just continued the search and continued asking and forming new relationships. For you sales and data-driven readers, if you use the metric of ten calls to get one meeting and ten meetings to get one sale, then you are headed into the right headspace.

It was when I had just finished listening to the latest podcast episode from the Drummers Resource created and curated by Nick Ruffini that I saw this quote stated so boldly on an Instagram post:

> *"If you can't find people who want to work with you, make your own opportunities to bring others to you!"*

Life changed! Mindset interrupted!

Regardless of your religious or spiritual beliefs, there are times that words, images, people, etc., are put in our path at a moment's time for a reason. A saying that I use quite often in conversation and that we should take quite seriously is "Time is not just a magazine." Well, this is most certainly no exception.

It seems these days, I have finally caught up to the rest of the songwriting world and have since switched to a more digital format for writing. I literally have access to all my song ideas immediately and can add to those ever-elusive song prompts, titles, and one-liners for when you walk into those co-writes. These sessions can be intimidating enough. Line after line, melodies, harmonies, and rhythms galore.

If you don't have Evernote, or a similar notes organization app or software, ask your friends or co-writers which ones they use. There are FREE apps. So, there are no excuses. Don't want to leave? Here are a few lines for you to write it out RIGHT NOW!

THREE SONG PROMPTS FOR YOUR NEXT WRITING SESSION

1. ____
2. ____
3. ____

Being able to just grab your device and dictate your notes and ideas immediately will save your brain hundreds of headaches later. When was the last time you sat in your office or on your couch spending time racking your brain on what you were so excited about earlier? It happened to me too often.

I was on a recent weekend tour with the Shane Martin Band, and since we had lots of windshield time and hotel downtime between the two nights of playing, it was the perfect opportunity for conversations and song ideas to show up. Shane and I were chatting, and in a moment, a line dropped. I said, "That's a killer song title," and then conversation just moved on. Guess what? I didn't write it down at that moment. The weekend tour came and went, and Monday morning, I was sitting in my office, racking my brain for almost an hour till I finally remembered it. Sure glad I did because that one line is going to be part of at least one song very soon here!

The joke in our house is that any list that includes more than two items must be written down on a physical list or in our shared shopping app. Also, it's a great way to teach your kids some "real life" skills and how even their parents don't have to try and remember everything.

Write that stuff down. We have enough distractions in our daily lives. And as you work through your creative process, you are going to find these ideas come flooding in multiple times a day.

Show up consistently and persistently, ready to work.

Ready to create. Adapt, change, move, shake, fail, get back up and be ready for the next door that opens. As we continue to work through what it even means to begin, the words of Thomas J. Watson, the founder and first CEO of IBM, should resonate through your head *"I'll fail my way to the top."*

Countless business connections, colleagues, friends, coaches, and acquaintances have become lifelong friends, brothers, and sisters, business partners, writing partners, collaborators, and connectors. The culmination of all these encounters and opportunities has led me to right here… staring at this screen…smack in the middle of the Road to 99.

By the time you're done reading this, I will have completed that 99th song goal! And yes, please do contact me and ask what song number I have now made it to. You might be surprised at what the response shall be!

Here, I'll make it easy for you:

Text: 320-420-2105

And yes, that IS my number, and please DO send me a message to ask! Sharing in the journey is the whole point. Whether it was to get you to even take your precious time to read this book or to share the songs with you along the way, your time is valuable. Invest it wisely.

With the uncertainty and yet immense clarity that has surrounded our worlds in the depths of 2020 and all that is the COVID-19 virus, it was fitting that collaboration, networking, and reaching farther than ever was the goal.

As you continue reading about this journey and experience and the nuts and bolts of some of the tactics, thoughts, and stories, make sure to take note and use the margins to help you document what you think your process was before and what it may look like now. YES, please write in this book.

My goal is that it would transform into something new. New for YOU. Not new for me, or your spouse, or your writing partners, your business partners, for YOU.

If you want someone to push you, guide you, and write with you, reach out at www.roadto99book.com and I'll hop write in! See what I did there…?

INSIDER TIP

Write a post on your Facebook page that you are looking for people to write with. See how many responses you get. Then follow up and make the writing happen!

WRITE

CHAPTER 3

IN THE BEGINNING

"You can't build a reputation on what you're going to do."
—Henry Ford

In the passing years, I've noticed some continuing patterns, themes, and newly arising opportunities that seem to have intertwined intricate connections and synapses. Sometimes merely a spark. Sometimes like the kindling in your campfire. Sometimes burning white-hot like the embers laying in a bed of coals. Whether spark or flame, ember, or ashes—all these started with two people and a moment of the first connection.

The brain is a VERY powerful muscle. But much like a muscle, it needs to be trained and given workouts, which create opportunities for it to grow and get stronger. Similarly, if you want to see your biceps and triceps take a muscular form, that is not just going to happen because you join CrossFit, Orangetheory Fitness, or Snap Fitness.

You must show up, do the workouts, feed your body with the right nutrients, and then after 30-40 days, you'll start to notice small physical changes. It's when you keep on going and hit days 50, 60, and 70 that the transformation truly begins to manifest itself. All that consistent work shines through. Not only that, but you've also created new habits, a new way of living, and most importantly—a new way of thinking.

This is a simple process. However, because of its simplicity, the steps are often overlooked. Successful businesses, musicians, and entrepreneurs are masters of the basics, the foundations, and the mundane.

- Show up.
- Move forward.
- Every day.
- Keep on showing up.
- Keep on coming back.
- Embrace the challenges.
- Embrace the roadblocks.

Meet them with open arms. Be consistent and persistent about moving around and through them. Obstacles are what you see when you take your eyes off the goal.

I often comment that most people leave their business one day before making it. It gets challenging; roadblocks continue to get in the way, and mastering the mundane becomes too much. They want to focus on big picture items. The vision they had, in the beginning when the spark was ignited, begins to feel like they are fading off into the distance like an ember blowing in the wind.

Know you are in it for the long game. It's a marathon. And like marathon runners, you must train—and train hard.

About five years ago, a chance crossing through Jaymi, who you met in the testimonials, had me sitting on my Cajon in the basement of Nate's home. For those who don't know, a Cajon is a rectangular box made from wood, with some wires and beads set into it so the player can create the sound and feel of a drum set. My goal on Cajon is to provide the energy, vibe, and sonic qualities one would expect when hearing a full drum set.

It's also interesting to me that this person lived only a few miles from where I grew up. Like many music and "band" projects, many times you show up and know only one of the musicians in the room.

And sometimes, NONE of them. All it takes is one small interaction or connection to get you in that room.

Some say nerve-wracking. I say opportunity. I love to embrace those moments. Although, if you've met me and seen my first interactions when I enter a room, you would most certainly label me as an introvert. And that would be quite accurate. No fear, the music pushes me out of that space for sure!

Chance meetings create opportunities to plant seeds. You then water those seeds over and over. The more often you have these interactions and spontaneous meetings, the more you have chances to build relationships. In these moments, you have no idea knowing when or what those relationships will grow into. Embrace that! And keep watering those seeds.

So, we all arrived at Nate's parents' house and headed down into their basement, where everyone else there already knew each other or had some sort of musical connection. Me, a wood box, a groove, and a chill vibe were the whole box of tricks I brought to the room that day. Honestly, I was scared to death! Remember, I'm an introvert, and that voice was screaming inside me right then. My small piece of solace comes from knowing deep down once the music begins, it will speak louder than anything else in the room. And no, I'm not just talking about the decibel level. With too many acoustic instruments and no amps, no way was it too loud. I'm referring to the musical contributions I was about to bring to the room. Remember, every interaction with you is one that will be unique and magical, too.

A song is the synergy of the musicians that are creating or performing it.

Though sometimes I joke with other bandmates (and even new musicians I've met along the way) that I know "all" the songs, there is most certainly some truth in that. Or as we say in the drumming world, "1 and 3, 2 and 4." Really, what else does there truly "need" to be. We, as drummers, are always playing a variation of that.

Small conversations and mere surface-level introductions were made, which were quickly followed by diving straight into the music. Three hours later, Jaymi, Johnny, and I all left and went our separate ways. I wasn't even gone 20 minutes, and Nate was already texting me, letting me know something cool had happened that day, and though he too wasn't sure what it meant or where it was headed, we knew it would be amazing.

As I drove my hour home, which was customary for me for most musical engagements, the windshield time brought one recurring theme, which was confirmed by that message, this...was only the beginning.

As fast as that project started, it was over. By over, I mean the band only momentarily known as "Fire Road" was over.

Although this seems like the world's shortest stint as a "band," this most definitely is all too often how it plays out. The crazy part was that there were already photos, a logo, and plans for booking venues. Create the product first, then put those plans into place.

Bands and musical projects are constantly starting, morphing, transforming, and disbanding. All too often, people forget that the music business is really the people business. It's relationships, it's emotions, it's gear, it's travel, late nights, for little or no pay—and it can be messy. Therefore, when you see bands that have been together for years, there is something magical that these musicians experienced and held onto. Or the alternative, they could just be bullheaded, and no one wants to be the one to end it. I'm guessing you've heard that version before.

If you're building a project for playing gigs, recording albums, or even touring, do some research about bands that have been around for a couple of decades. Study them; what are some of the steps they took, and what were some of the obstacles they ran into? The Rolling Stones, RUSH, The Eagles, Zac Brown Band, Dave Matthews Band, The Beatles, and The Police are some great places to start your research.

Well, that day started Nate and me on a journey neither of us could have predicted. Over the next couple of years, our paths continued to cross, each time adding a little more water to those seeds, providing further growth for what was to come. Sometimes it was as simple as being at the same music venues together and just saying hi. More often, it was a chance to hang out, talking about our musical journeys up to that point.

Water those seeds because opportunities, leads, connections, and relationships can only become fruitful if you take action.

I believe you are about to experience in just one case how that can play out.

Winstock Country Music Festival is one of the biggest country music festivals in MN, and Nate came and hung out in the media area where I was camping. I was playing on a couple of stages that year with a regional country band called Mitch Gordon & The Unleaded Band. We spent hours each day and late into both evenings just talking about life, the music industry, and exploring the options of how we could work together. We both had been in bands and experienced different versions and seen dozens of our friends go through varying versions of touring.

WE wanted something different.
WE wanted to show up differently.
WE wanted to carve a different path.

So, WE did. We kept building and deepening our conversation in the ensuing months. We took small opportunities to discover new possibilities and work out new options of how to plow our path forward.

And then, after a few years, he moved away to Music City, Nashville, following an opportunity to be a merchandising manager for a country acapella group. Sometimes the idea of something you were working to build can suddenly feel as if it has ended. Like it has come to a screeching halt. NOT ME! My reaction was one of excitement!!

Excitement? How many musicians or business owners do you know who celebrate when they see what seems like a failed endeavor? I did. We did. It was for the best and absolutely what was needed.

Where one door seems like it closes, one is most certainly going to open.

That following summer, I found myself boarding a plane to Nashville for the first time and crashing at his place. Don't worry. I'll get to the story about how I got there a little later, as that is a seed-planting tale in and of itself.

Old school bandmate style. One-bedroom apartment with a small kitchen table, a few couches, no TV, and a screaming loud air conditioning unit. I'm not sure if you've ever been in Nashville in the middle of July, but that is an essential part of comfort when the temps hit 95-100 and 95% humidity.

I slept on a couch that was too short for me, stayed up late listening to music, and met the dozens of musicians down on Broadway. Again, more time to integrate our music and business ideas as we moved forward.

Sleeping in. Well, Nate slept in. Taking afternoon naps and repeating. Back then, it was a favorite part of his day.

Part of that was true. I spent countless hours scheduling meetings after meetings with other musicians, drummers, songwriters, music producers, and studio owners. You want to talk about planting seeds...it was like a freshly plowed field in the spring ready for its crop. I couldn't wait to put those seeds in the ground. Then water them over and over on the ensuing trips.

Those first couple of times down to Nashville were inspiring, a LOT of work, and beyond rewarding! I knew if I was going to, on a regular basis, take that time to leave my family, I was going to be putting in as many hours of interactions with people as they were available.

AND THIS was the beginning of our songwriting and music-creating journey! Our Road to 99!

INSIDER TIP

A journey can only begin if you take the first step. Think about five people you want to reach out to right now and start planting those seeds.

CHAPTER 4

THE WRITING SESSIONS

"One day, in retrospect, the years of struggle
will strike you as the most beautiful."
—Sigmund Freud

A good friend asked me a question a few years ago when I started talking about songwriting. He asked, "Are you really a songwriter if you aren't writing songs all the time?"

Just reading the words "writing session" can give some writers an anxiety attack. Hold onto your thoughts as you hear some of the ups and downs and ins and outs of how many of the sessions Nate and I played out. They just might strike a chord with you.

Songwriting is a verb. It's action. It's doing.

Our first writing sessions began by sitting down at the kitchen table with two low-ball glasses and a bottle of whiskey. Two guys, a guitar, and a vision.

Write, record, and release music out to the world.

Those first few nights of writing sure turned into some very early mornings. Building trust, building a vocabulary, and working through what and where our process could at least begin.

Trust me. This was not when we figured out any sort of sustainable process. The important part at that stage was that we were doing it and beginning to put in the work. I think those first couple of songs took us two or three evenings each! In many songwriting circles, they would consider that a win. Back then, I'm sure we did as well.

Let's face it; we were having fun! Music is supposed to be fun! Building something from the ground up, even if you are still just in the discovery and research phase, still needs to be fun. Life's too short, and we were about to put in thousands of hours of work, so we stayed focused on that.

Compared to the pace we write at currently, we were working at a sloth's speed for sure. However, back then, we didn't have the commitment level and buy-in to make it happen in any other way. All too often, in the beginning, you don't yet know what you don't know. Just keep going.

As quickly as we began, our momentum was halted. Both of our lives got busy, and my trips increased to Nashville. However, Nate's travels also heavily increased, and many times, he wasn't even home when I was down there.

It's important to note that the trips didn't stop, the communication didn't stop, and though we couldn't always be in the same space, we kept our vision of writing, recording, and releasing music at the forefront of our conversations.

And then COVID-19 hit the world.

Yes.

Here is a timestamp in history. March 13th, 2019.

On May 14th, 2019, we found ourselves reconnected after I pitched the idea that we start writing over Zoom. Imagine the money that Zoom made and the explosion of business they gained from this one event. Our process had a similar boom for sure.

I had already been collaborating with another writer, Mark Stone, on Zoom for a few months, and I knew we could make it work for us.

Not going to lie; it took a little convincing and selling to make Nate a believer. So, we tried it a few times, and once we both had a good comfort level, we committed to doing it weekly. Thus, the birth of our Tuesday morning writing sessions. As a creative, it seems as though we should come up with a name for these sessions. If you have any great ideas, send them my way!

In a recent writing session, we found ourselves talking about the day's events, what happened last week, and so forth. Which, let's face it: most writing sessions begin with some sort of conversation, therapy session, or hanging out. Then we started jotting down lines and working on the subject for the song for that session. Three verses and two choruses in, and we realized this was nowhere near the direction we thought it would take that day.

Seems like the most invigorating and satisfying writing sessions end up this way.

We get out of our own way and let the music do the talking.

We become the vessel through which music speaks and enters the world. That Tuesday morning session was also where we came up with the simplest chorus, easiest chord changes, and the longest song we had written to date! We did a double-take when we looked at the screen as we were about to record the work tape and discovered that it truly was a very simple song. Yet I had to keep the mouse scrolling down the screen so Nate could play and sing through it. It was one of the longer songs we had written!

Notice I said that we recorded it. Yep, you guessed it, it goes right inside Evernote, allowing us to share the notes and make changes in real-time. Using this app also gave the session a feeling of being in the same room together.

October 20th, 2020, and we were on song 25 for the year! That's a whole lot of twenties! Here's to manifesting some real 20-dollar bills from all these songs. I'm not completely sold on this as an idea. However, if ten pounds of twenty-dollar bills decided to hit my doorstep, that would certainly be one for the win column.

I find it also ironic that the title of that song turned out to be "Going Out of My Head." Don't worry; we also had a good laugh about that.

It seemed quite fitting because, at this point, we were going a little out of our heads. Part of us couldn't believe that we were continuing to write songs at this pace. It was not just the pace but the ability to be consistent. Especially as we spoke with other writing friends of ours and many of them struggled to write a handful of songs each year.

A question still haunted me, nagging my brain as we had started writing songs. Are we really songwriters? What does that even mean?

As I defined it, a songwriter is:

A person who shows up consistently, writes songs with others or on their own, records them in some fashion, and then releases them for the world to hear.

I believe the magic in the above definition lies in the first part, a person who "shows up consistently." Doing the work over and over persistently and consistently.

WE SHOW UP!

Nate and I made an agreement to keep each other in check and keep the focus and mission on the process of writing continuously, also to delay the recording process until we had some fuel to put on the fire, which would then initiate the process of recording. This gave us the opportunity to stay focused on the writing. It may be cliché, but so many songwriters want to put on the 10,000-person festivals before they've even done a demo recording on their phone with an idea.

You may be slightly confused by this process. Especially those of you reading who are not musicians (thank you for reading, by the way). Or maybe you are even asking yourself *why don't you record and release every song you write?*

Think of it as like a funnel. You load a bunch into the top, and not all of them make it to the bottom. Some might sit in the funnel a lot longer and need some time to work themselves down to the bottom. Some don't even make it to the recording and releasing phases. They were just there to help you get to the next song, acting as building blocks and opportunities to discover new ways to put lyrics, melodies, and rhythms together.

There are even times that songs make it to the recording phase but never get released. It's interesting that this happens quite often for some musicians. It could be for several reasons: budget, fear, band broke up, no supporting tour, or just didn't find enough value in them after creating them. These are still at-bats in the recording column. And you need those, too!

Much like a writer who makes hundreds of edits and revisions of their book, exactly like what I have done in this book, it takes time to edit and craft a song into the right version of itself. Sometimes, like several of the ones we've written so far, they might not resonate with us enough to want to create anything more out of them.

Something magical happens when you find a song you've just written that resonates with you. Suddenly, you start to hear all the other parts. You can hear in your head how the drum groove will go and where the bass guitar may enter to compliment and bring that groove alive. Then you hear the vocal coming into the mix and the interaction and conversation it has with the other lead instruments all sitting on top of a wonderful bed of some rhythmic motion from the guitars or maybe even keys. More about this later when we talk specifically about the recording process.

You do have to fill the funnel. We think of it as "fueling the fire." Some people call it putting gas in the tank. This is quite appropriate as the name we came up with for this dynamic duo of creation is, The Dumpsterfire. *Hope you got a little chuckle out of that, as well.* I mean, 2020 was eloquently labeled as the Dumpsterfire Year, and they even made a Christmas ornament dedicated to it.

Keep on writing.
Keep on creating.
Keep on showing up.

See a theme forming? As we moved from song 9 to song 17, to song 31, to song 55, to song 67, we kept our thought process the same and just kept on writing.

Let's take a walk through some of the blocks of songs along our journey, where I felt like we experienced some changes in the process, shifts in our mindset, or how we approached the sessions as we continued down our Road to 99.

INSIDER TIP

Spend the next 30 days just writing one line of a lyric per day. They don't have to have anything to do with each other. Just one line per day.

SONGWRITING SESSIONS AND EXAMPLES

CHAPTER 5

WE ALL BEGIN SOMEWHERE

"Every artist was first an amateur."
—Ralph Waldo Emerson

SONGS 1-15

We now call this collection of writing sessions the garbage sessions. I mean, we all begin somewhere. And no, the project name Dumpsterfire was in place long before we even started these sessions.

Everyone has their first song. You might even have dozens of first songs. In those beginning stages, you are making all sorts of attempts at figuring out a process. If you remember, I filled a few notebooks with song lyrics before I even started writing with others.

The next few sections build upon each other, and I have included some lyric selections from the noted song numbers along our journey. In full disclosure, the selected lyric examples are of songs we haven't recorded or released. Remember, songs take longer to percolate in the funnel sometimes. Or maybe it was just the next song to learn something from and then build upon the skills and knowledge gained.

I think this is much more indicative of how many songs you need to build into your library, whether they are recorded in a releasable format or not. We must work through these beginning songs, knowing the opportunity, in the beginning, is few and far between.

Embrace the process and enjoy building the habits and the basic skills to even make a co-write go well.

There is also something nostalgic and insightful about going back and looking and listening through these beginning ones. Some of them we don't necessarily even have work tapes for. Which is a big loss, and it makes it interesting to go back and think about them.

Although in those beginning months, it took a lot of effort to just show up every Tuesday morning. We'd both made the commitment, yet we would watch our phones on Monday nights to see if the other one would cancel. Then dread being up so early to do a writing session at 8 am.

It was a commitment. We committed to the process and helped each other stay accountable. Building each other up and being willing to push each other to keep going. Even if some days we would both show up tired, overworked, and stressed. This was when our sessions began with our brains in another space. We needed to get them back in the game. I can certainly say there were times it was a 50/50 split on whose brain may have needed help. However, I am thankful I had a co-writing partner who wanted to go the distance and was willing to speak into that for me.

Find co-writers or creative partners who are willing to speak to you where you are at. Being critical of each other, offering feedback on events and conversations outside of writing, and being a support system creates an even stronger connection. Trust me; this leads to the songs flowing out even easier.

In the coming pages and each section following, I am going to give you examples of exactly how our notes look in Evernote. You'll see the arrangement, the chords, the lyrics, and the logistics of the track. In the note, we also include that work tape from the actual session, so we have the audio reference of the melodic and rhythmic elements.

INSIDER TIP

Don't worry about creating a number one hit song. You are there to start and finish a song in the session.

SONG 6 – "LIKE IT WAS YESTERDAY" JUNE 17TH, 2020

Intro: Em (4x's)

Verse 1: C B7 Em Em (2x's)
Walking down the street
When a stranger looks our way
Flipping through the script
And everything is gonna stay
That feline is running
And hasn't been home in awhile
Searching for a text
That's been lost somewhere in denial

Chorus: G B C Em G B C Cm
Woah oh oh oh oh
oh oh oh oh oh
Woah oh oh oh oh
oh oh oh oh oh...

Verse 2:
Out in the world
Been looking for a place to stay
Dropped all the marbles
Watched them all walk away
Tried to call a cab
But the operator's gone
It's an island view
Depends what side you're on

Chorus: G B C Em G B C Cm
Woah oh oh oh oh
oh oh oh oh oh
Woah oh oh oh oh
oh oh oh oh oh...

Verse 3: (Broke Down) C B7 Em Em C B7 Cm.......
Running down the street
When a stranger looks our way
Burning through the script
Like it was yesterday

Double Chorus: G B C Em G B C (A C) (B7 last time)
Woah oh oh oh oh
oh oh oh oh oh
Woah oh oh oh oh
oh oh oh oh oh...

SONG 12 – "NEVER WANTED ANYTHING MORE"
JULY 24TH, 2020

Intro: ||: A G :|| A G

Verse 1: ||: A G :|| A G G D
She's on fire
Ya she's burning down the town
She's a liar
Packed full of energy and
Desire
She's driving all over
Leave you stone cold sober
And you've never wanted anything more! ....

Verse 2:
It's alright
Don't need to tuck her in at
Night
T-T-Tops rolled down
Out of sight
Everything you're thinking's
Gonna leave you blinking
And you've never wanted anything more!

Chorus: E G D
Everything you're thinking's
Gonna leave you blinking
And you've never wanted anything more!

TA: ||:A G :|| 4x's

Solo: ||: D G D G :|| E ....

Shout: ||: A G :|| A G
She's on Fire
She's a liar
It's alright
Out of Sight

Chorus: E G D
And you've never wanted anything
Never wanted anything
You've never wanted anything

TA: ||: A G :|| 2x's

Solo: ||: D G D G :|| E ....

Outro: ||:A G :|| (vamp)
And you've never wanted anything
Never wanted anything
You've never wanted anything

CHAPTER 6

THE HONEYMOON PHASE

"Art is something that makes you breathe
with a different kind of happiness."
—Anni Albers

SONGS 16-35

Put in the work. Keep on pushing. At this stage, you are entering what I would call the "honeymoon phase" of writing. You are still excited every time you leave your house, hop on a Zoom screen, or pick up that pen. Everything feels good and comfortable, and everyone's happy.

I met my friend Brendan during the pandemic through a mutual friend and, it again, was one of those moments of immediate connection. He brought to my attention that working remotely together really can feel as smooth as sitting right there in the same room. So don't be afraid to work with creatives across the globe!

Bring your daily encounters to the session. You never know what will be the spark that will bring the small amount of fuel you need to light the writing fire. Sometimes, it's just a word, sometimes a small phrase, or maybe even something that came up in the conversation you were having prior to diving in.

Many times, I'll even look at what's in the background. It can be that simple. Take that writing hack to your next session. Whether it's a word from a poster on the wall, of something someone in the background says, or an inspiration from a conversation taking place next to you.

Corporations have spent hundreds, thousands, and in some cases millions of dollars to come up with the right design, look, concept, message, etc. They went through the grueling creative process already; you might as well put that to work for you.

Here are a few examples that came up for us:

1. Cat's in the bag
2. Living the dream
3. Can on the shelf
4. Whiskey in my glass
5. I've had enough
6. Get me off this bus
7. California sunrise
8. Get me out of here
9. Last chance

What are five words or phrases you can come up with right now inside the space you are in?

1. ______________________________
2. ______________________________
3. ______________________________
4. ______________________________
5. ______________________________

Keep your eyes and ears always open! Here's a hint: have a page in your Notes app or voice memo on your phone and jot down or quickly record them and save them. You are ambushed by marketing and advertisements daily. Trust me; you can find some inspiration through all the visual and auditory assaults. You just must be open, aware, and intentional.

When we first began, I started a Notes page and committed to adding at least one lyrical line to it every day. Just that one simple thirty-second commitment every day turned into 30 new ideas at the end of the month. Bring just a couple of those ideas into a writing room and see what happens. It is likely to spark an idea in others you could have never dreamed of. And at that moment, they spit out an entire verse! I continue to add to and sift through these ideas even years later.

Take my earlier example about my weekend conversation with Shane; that one line leads to an entire song with another collaborator.

During this phase, we felt ourselves getting into a solid groove. It was about the time we hit song 25 that we started to notice a change in our mindsets about Tuesday mornings. It was now the favorite part about both of our weeks. Showing up wasn't even an option. It was expected, and we couldn't wait. You could feel the joy, excitement, and positive energy beginning to flow through those sessions.

It became a bit of a game between the two of us to see who would text the other first about the upcoming Tuesday morning. Many times, I told my high school students, "Music is supposed to be fun, and it's even more fun when you are good." So just keep working on it and focus on getting better each time. We did. We showed up, did the work, had lots of laughs, and continued writing.

At this point, we started sending each other lyric excerpts and little guitar ditties to think about throughout the week—giving each other small nuggets to keep our brains in creative mode all week. Honestly, sometimes these just fell by the wayside, and we might not have even talked about them. However, it did keep the energy going. The good part is they are still in my notes, and I can return to them at any time.

You could also agree that this was a way to keep each other moving in a positive direction all week. Having a partner in creation can also be paralleled as a workout or accountability partner. This is someone who will make sure you show up each week and who makes sure your headspace is clear and filled with some positive energy each day.

Get creative this week and just send someone a positive note or a thought for them to think about a couple of times. See what kind of effect it begins to have on them. Maybe you even just send a song you are listening to. You'd be surprised at how many times the person on the other end of that message really needed that song at that moment.

I was meeting with a coaching client of mine recently, and she shared a powerful story with me about how she is still, today, using a social media post that I made a year ago. The post was about the power and presence of music in our lives and how it brings back so many emotions and experiences from our past.

Just listening to a song that comes from a point in time, an experience, or a life event can bring a physical and mental feeling like we are right back there.

She shared that the reading of the post serendipitously landed near the anniversary of her sister's sudden passing. She took that thought, put it into action, and shared songs she loved to listen to with her sister and their friends, AND continues to share those songs with her family and friends annually to celebrate those memories of joy, laughter, and connection with her sister.

Imagine the power those songs are having on people. And YOU, as the writer, producer, or artist, don't even have an idea of the impact you made.

Keep writing!

Are you looking for someone to collaborate remotely with?

Hit me up! Let's make some music!

Send me a text: 320-420-2105, and I'll send you a one-liner or two to get you going or inspire you as you head into your upcoming writing sessions. Then make a video of your work, and post it on your favorite social media outlet with the #Roadto99OneLiner so I can find it and enjoy your journey.

INSIDER TIP

Use all your senses as opportunities to help you brainstorm ideas. In case you forgot those from back in pre-school, here's the list: smell, touch, see, hear, and taste.

SONG 18 – "LONELY DAYS"
SEPTEMBER 29TH, 2020

Intro: C#m (4x's)

Verse 1: C#m G#m A B
What's outside
Staring back at me
And the raindrops
Run into my eyes

Verse 2: C#m G#m A B
What's inside
Staring out at you
But the pain
Will never die

Chorus: F#m A E G#m F#m B
Lonely days
Lonely days
Lonely days
Are on the rise

TA: C#m (4x's)

Verse 3:
It's been awhile
Since you were born
Now you're walking
Taller than before

Verse 4:
Once in awhile
But before I go
The rain
Will wash away the earth

Chorus: F#m A E G#m F#m B
Lonely days
Lonely days
Lonely days
Are on the rise

TA: C#m (4x's)

Solo: C#m B A E (2x's)

Chorus: F#m A E G#m F#m B
Lonely days
Lonely days
Lonely days (pause)
Are on the rise

Outro: C#m
On the rise
On the rise
On the rise
On the rise (rit.)

SONG 29 – "WIN LOSE OR DRAW"
DECEMBER 8TH, 2020

Intro: A G A F A C D (2x's)

Verse 1: A G A F A C D
Trapped
In a town with no name
Exits all around me
With no one left to blame
Stacked
With deuces all around
A gun can only save you
If your feet don't touch the ground

Chorus: ||: F C G :|| (down)
Win Lose or Draw
Sometimes you have it all
Win Lose or Draw

Verse 2: A G A F A C D (Em)
Jokers all around me
The smile's on my face
Double down without a crown
Shooting up the place
Smoking down the highway
It's nowhere 65
Breathing
Just trying to stay alive

Chorus: ||: F C G :|| F C G Bb G Em (Full)
Win Lose or Draw
Sometimes you have it all
Win Lose or Draw
Sometimes you can't stop the fall
Win Lose or Draw
Just gotta keep moving on
Cause Win lose or draw

Solo: A G A F A F G (4x's)

Chorus: ||: F C G :|| F C G (1/2 time)
Win Lose or Draw
Sometimes you have it all
Win Lose or Draw
Sometimes you can't stop the fall
Win Lose or Draw
Just gotta keep moving on

Chorus: ||: F C G :|| F C G Bb F G (Full)
Win Lose or Draw
Sometimes you have it all
Win Lose or Draw
Sometimes you can't stop the fall
Win Lose or Draw
Just gotta keep moving on
Cause Win lose or draw

Outro: A G A F A C D (Fade out)

CHAPTER 7
THE GRIND

"The chief enemy of creativity is 'good' sense."
—Pablo Picasso

SONGS 36-50

Keep showing up. You might be surprised when you take a moment to look up, and your songs are really starting to stack up. One might even begin to say they have a collection.

YOU are building your library.

As we moved into this pile of songs, we began talking about what it might look like to start recording some of these songs. Notice we arrived at this conversation once we were 36 songs in. We started feeling like what we were writing was worthy of sharing. You must be a little careful with that statement of "worthy" since it's hard to know what listeners will think until you get them out there. We took the view that we maybe had something to say.

There are certainly times in the lives of songwriters when they are writing songs just to write songs. And then there are times when what they are saying lyrically and through the music has a deeper meaning. They are looking to dig deeper into their creative soul and share that with their audience, which gives them a glimpse into the writer's eye.

What could have changed as we got to this point? It has to do with the sheer volume and the amount of "at-bats" that we had. We could work through tough conversations. We could turn each other down on the lyrics or the direction of the song.

These can be very tough conversations and thoughts to bring up in a session. Marty Dodson, Clay Mills, and Bill O'Hanlon, in their book, *The Songwriter's Guide to Mastering Co-Writing*, talk about using phrases like:

- *Yes, and...*
- *I'm just not feeling that idea. Let's keep digging until we find one we both love.*
- *I LOVE that! What if we take it in this direction?*
- *What if...*

We were also pushing each other to expand and dig deeper when we found something worthy. Don't shy away from those conversations. If you do, at some point, they are going to inhibit the creative flow, and you might miss out on something amazing by not speaking up.

You also risk the opportunity to lose a writing partner by not being honest and having the opportunity to be vulnerable.

When I am performing live with a group of musicians I know very well, we will make the joke back and forth, saying, "I really like what you were trying to do there." Read that a few times and let it sink in. Maybe it will come in handy for you at some point this week.

Song #40 was written on March 2nd, 2021, and we found it to be quite hilarious that we titled it "Let It All Soak In." As we sat, reminiscing about the first 39, we let the words start to flow, followed by a few strums of the guitar to lay out a groove and chord structure. And finally, a hook and the arrangement of the song. They seemed to pour out again and again. Each time we took more and more risks and stretched even with the simplest of chord structures. It's as though the songs just poured over onto the page.

Let's take a moment and think about that idea of letting it all soak in. It's important to take moments and talk about the actual process and how you can accomplish large volumes of material in these sessions. More on reflection later; however, as it is part of the process, you will start to notice and be aware of it along the way and constantly cycle back to it.

We still sit and chuckle about those evenings years ago when we first wrote together and thought it took late nights and sipping whiskey just to write something "good" or worthy of listeners.

I find that this is a theme that many artists and musicians can certainly fall victim to. The brain on the high of music is literally loaded with dopamine, giving it that natural feeling of a "high." This is why you often see great musicians of the past turn to sex and drugs once they are not working in music full-time. They are trying to recreate and relive those moments of the musical high you get from being on stage and playing live in front of people or spending long days and nights in the recording studio.

This happens with musicians at the top of the game, who are touring large arenas and stadiums and trickles all the way down to those who work the local club scene as a "weekend warrior," so to speak. The brain doesn't differentiate between the number of people who may be watching the performance. It merely knows that the musician is playing an instrument and is taking in the rest of the sounds and textures from the musicians around them.

As we continued writing, we found ourselves saying every other week that we "really liked that one." "Let's record that one." To be quite honest, we are still doing that! That's what makes the process so exciting. Trust me; if we had an unlimited budget and a studio full of musicians all the time, we most likely would be doing that.

That is most certainly what we are both working toward. It takes time and lots of effort and continuing to show up. The synergy that you can create and the compounded efforts of energy that work toward those common goals make it just seem inevitable.

We WILL make it happen.
We WILL arrive at that place.
We WILL see this through to the end.

INSIDER TIP

Just showing up every week is exactly the inspiration your co-writer needs. They rely on you. You rely on them.

SONG 33 – "BLUE SMOKEY MONDAY"
JANUARY 8TH, 2020

Intro: ||: E A F#m B :||

Verse 1: ||: E A F#m B :|| E A B C#m A B
It's a blue smokey Monday
Oh ah oh
We made it past Sunday
Oh ah oh
It seems alright
It seems alright
But we're back
Where we came from
We've been wrong all along

TA: ||: E A F#m B :||

Verse 2: ||: E A F#m B :|| E A B C#m A B

Out on the freeway
Oh ah oh
Dreaming 'bout a way
Oh ah oh
It seems alright
It seems alright
As we leave
Where we came from
We've been wrong all along
We've been wrong all along

Bridge: C#m A C#m F#m C#m A C#m F#m B

Verse Tag: E A B F#m B
It seems alright
It seems alright
As we leave
Where we came from

Verse 3: ||: E A F#m B :|| E A B C#m A B
Everything a stray
Oh ah oh
Guess it's just that way
Oh ah oh
It seems alright
It seems alright
We return
Where we came from
We've been wrong all along

Outro:
We've been wrong all along
We've been wrong all along
We've been wrong all along

SONG 45 – "OUT THERE"
MAY 5TH, 2021

Extended Intro: D C G (12-16x's)

Chorus: D C G (broken down)
Still playing in a rock n roll band
Detroit city to the Rio Grande
Still trying to find the rock n roll fans
Out there

TA: D C G

Verse 1: D C G
Bob Seger's
Stuck on the radio in my head
While the band
Still feels like half past dead

TA: D C G

Verse 2: D C G
Citizens
United in the world by love
Innocence
Taking flight like the mourning dove

Chorus: D C G A
Still playing in a rock n roll band
Detroit city to the Rio Grande
Still trying to find the rock n roll fans
Out there

Solo: D C G (8x's)

Verse 3: D C G
Standin'
On a corner in Tennessee
There's a girl, My Lord
In a black bed Ford
Speeding up to stop lookin' at me

Chorus: D C G
Still playing in a rock n roll band
Detroit city to the Rio Grande
Still trying to find the rock n roll fans
Out there

Dbl Chorus: D C G A
Still playing in a rock n roll band
Detroit city to the Rio Grande
Still trying to find the rock n roll fans
Out there
TA: D C G

Outro Chorus: (cities list)
New York City, Nazareth, PA
Monticello, Goodlettsville, TN

CHAPTER 8

ARE WE THERE YET?

"Have no fear of perfection. You'll never reach it."
—Salvador Dali

SONGS 51-67

This is every parent's worst nightmare of a statement. *Are we there yet?* It's instilling that value of continuing to show up. Be present and part of the discussion.

From 940 miles away, over the view and audio of a computer screen, we laugh, we converse, we write, we CREATE! EVERY WEEK! Relentless in the pursuit of continually creating and working on our craft to become the best versions of ourselves and driving the impact of our collaboration.

By writing what's in the room and pulling from those ideas, the song becomes more universal and understandable to a vast listening audience. Two of us are bringing stories to the room; we use them and find creative ways to mash them into each other. This created a stronger and more tightly knit message inside the song.

As songwriters, it's important for us to stop and think about who our audience will be. Or who we envision them to be. This gives us an idea as to whether the lyrical direction is one where the listener can fill in their own blanks in the story. Or if we want to be deliberate and tell them every detail.

We continued to have a recurring theme of the music just lending itself to speaking through us. One might say the music was "in us," and we just needed to use the energy from each other to pull it out.

Does this mean we have figured something out? Again, I'd say it just leads to more questions.

And then there are those moments where you find yourself taking a few weeks off. We did. Babies are born. Family trips are taken. Many times, life just happens. Go with the flow. Be there to support each other and keep the forward motion happening, the conversations going, and give your co-writers space if they need it.

As an introvert, sometimes "I" am the one who simply needs that break. Caves can be great places to find inspired and new creative ideas. If you're an introvert, you know exactly what I'm talking about.

During those weeks off or the vacations, keep notes of your experiences, and take a moment to jot down ideas so you can return to the sessions with a pile of material to sort through. I'm guessing you own a smart device and can also take photos and document your experiences, vacations, and time away. Those, too, can become sources of creative material. They give you something to talk about; you can flesh out themes and come up with new lyrical content.

Side note…this also makes great content for when you begin talking about recording and releasing! "Show" your listeners where your ideas came from. Give them a sneak peek into how the creative process led you to that song.

There IS one other option.
TAKE THE TIME OFF!

It IS important as creatives that we take time off and don't live every moment constantly straining our brain and emotions to create and come up with something new.

I have found that in those moments of pause, I return to my creative sessions with more ideas, more enthusiasm, and a renewed spirit for the creative process. We "know" we are supposed to take breaks. I am here giving you the permission that you may not be able to give yourself.

INSIDER TIP

Smile. Yes, smile. You are writing songs.
You'll be amazed at the power of such a simple gesture.

SONG 59 – "JUST RIDE"
SEPTEMBER 14TH, 2021

Intro: Bm G A A (2x's)

Verse 1: Bm G A A
Take the bounty and run
Like you've never run before
Just follow the sun
But don't start the war

Pre-Chorus: Bm G A A
If your gun's undecided
You're not alone
You know the writing's
On the wall

Chorus: D G A A D G A A
Ride Cowboy ride
Into the deeper side (into the deeper side)
Ride Cowboy ride
Just ride
...

Verse 2: Bm G A A
You never saw anyone
You didn't wanna help
Now they're all gone
And it's all a sign

Pre-Chorus: Bm G A A
If your heart's undecided
You're not alone
You know the writing's
On the wall

Chorus: D G A A D G A A
Ride Cowboy ride
Into the deeper side (into the deeper side)
Ride Cowboy ride
All the time
Ride Cowboy ride
Just ride

Solo: Bm G A A (2x's)

Chorus: D G A A D G A A
Ride Cowboy ride
Into the deeper side (into the deeper side)
Ride Cowboy ride
All the time (All the time)
Ride Cowboy ride
Into the deeper side (into the deeper side)
Ride Cowboy ride
All the time
Ride Cowboy ride
Just ride
...

Outro: Bm G A A (fade out)

SONG 64 – "UNTIL YOU'RE RIGHT"
DECEMBER 14TH, 2021

Intro: D (4x's)

Verse 1: D D G D A A D D
We'll be wrong until you're right
Nobody's arguing tonight
War is probably insight
We'll be wrong until you're right

Verse 2: D D G D A A D D
We'll be wrong until you're right
Singing country songs tonight
Songs I don't really like
We'll be wrong until you're right

Bridge: Em A Em A A
It's all living in your head
It's all living in your head

Solo: D D G D A A D D

Verse 3: D D G D A A D D
We'll be wrong until you're right
Drinking under neon lights
Pull me over cuff me tight
We'll be wrong until you're right

Verse 4: D D G D A A D D
We'll be wrong until you're right

We're just trying to keep it light
You're a dick and that's a fact
So why don't you get off my back

GRAND PAUSE

Bridge: Em A Em A A //
It's all living in your head
It's all living in your head

Solo: D D G D A A D D

Mindset And Movement

CHAPTER 9

MINDSET AND MOVEMENT

"If you don't write your own script,
the world will write it for you."
—Chase Jarvis

We don't "allow" ourselves to be stuck in a single space. What do I mean by that? We don't put ourselves in a "genre" box or a particular feeling or mood. It usually begins with some sort of word, phrase, chord patterns, or rhythmic feel. That's how ANY song would start.

Which is exactly my point. We just START. AND then go one step further. We understand the importance of knowing that the goal is to finish. And finish WE DO!

Each session ends with putting down a little work tape demo on our phones. Thank God for voice memos and lots of available space on today's smartphones. They make checking back when we ask, "How did that one go?" much easier after a few months or even a year.

So, one might say that the only parameter that we put on our writing sessions is the length of time we lock into our calendar every week. And with Nate, we spend two hours per week. This means a guaranteed song every week! All we focus on is continuing to show up.

Each…and…every…week!

Commit to the process, commit to showing up, commit to continually growing and expanding your ideas and methods you take to approach each session.

We don't allow ourselves to decide if it's a good song, a bad song, or a song no one will like.

We continually ask ourselves if anyone will even ever hear them. Out of the current 65, we have chosen a small handful that we even want to move forward with the pre-production process. But more about how that process lays out in the next section.

My mindset was such that I wanted it to be about the process and that I had *"already done it"* rather than *"hey, look at this new thing that I am doing."* SO many times, I see runners, writers, artists saying, "Hey, look at me; I did this thing." My follow-up question is usually, "Okay, and now what? What else do you have? More songs? How many more miles?"

INSIDER KNOWLEDGE:

Music executives and record labels are now saying the same thing. Many of them don't start with the "up-and-coming" artists on the list. They want to see that they have done it, are doing it, and have systems in place already, instead of lighting the fire and getting it going for the artist. They are seen more as the barrels of gasoline that get poured onto the already blazing fire.

Get a good pen that flows well. Have a notebook with you EVERYWHERE you go. Even having the notebook with you will prompt you into ideas.

For example, you're driving in your car, and the notebook goes sliding across the passenger seat. As you attempt to grab it before it falls onto the snow-filled carpet floor below, you sit up promptly and make sure you gain control of the car and wait until you've stopped to reach over and grab it again.

Quick! Write down three thoughts that just went through your head that you can come back to later:

1. ____
2. ____
3. ____

Be intentional.
Be consistent and persistent.
Make it a daily activity.
This isn't just your new habit. It's a new way of living.

So, step into that action. As you can see, I set up standing weekly appointments, and they are repeated week after week, which makes that part easy. I'm asked time and time again how I manage all these pieces, and the answer is quite simple. I live by my calendar, and everything flows through there.

Here's something to get on your calendar...

...your writing session, project, or coaching call with me! Head over to www.RoadTo99Book.com and start your journey today.

INSIDER TIP

Having a mentor is essential to your growth. Whether the coach is helping you with your mindset, your writing, or the growth of your business, use their path as a guide in learning what things you can skip!

CHAPTER 10

GROW IN THE PROCESS

"Leaders think and talk about the solutions.
Followers think and talk about the problems."
—Brian Tracy

It was inside that grind, the consistent and persistent showing up, where the beginning framework for Road to 99 was born. Certainly, it seems fitting that you can relate it to a child growing up. It begins at birth, as it starts in its infancy, the daily and constant moments of growth and positive movement push it forward.

Newborn babies grow at such a rapid rate, even if it seems like nothing is taking place. Constantly taking in sights and sounds that they have NEVER experienced. They are doubling their intake each day. Many parents might even say they triple or quadruple their intake and growth each day.

Since 85% of our brains are formed by the time we are three, you can see how much information we are taking in and are trying to digest, learn, and store for future use. It is as though the music creativity was constantly growing inside—taking in new ideas, thoughts, genres, ways of thinking, and creating music.

Much like toddlers and learning the art of speaking, we need to constantly be around adults, mentors, and other writers, learning from our mistakes. Yes, that does mean you will make mistakes—and you should.

The more you are around these mentors, coaches, and creative professionals, the quicker you will elevate your skills. Reach out to me. I'll write a song with you!! Think of it like one of my favorite moments from the movie *Top Gun*. It's when Maverick is opening his orders at the final graduation party, and his instructor, Viper, says,

> *"Maverick, you'll get your RIO when you get to the ship. And if you don't, give me a call. I'll fly with you."*

Like a toddler, one eventually begins to crawl and do some exploration on their own. Even though they will still stay within proximity to their parents, they are expanding that distance and reaching farther on their own. These explorations might be a lonely road; they may just be with the next person who has come into your circle. It might be a new teammate or employee who has just started and is bringing in all sorts of creative ideas.

As that crawling becomes more comfortable and the need to be attached lessens, we begin to walk. Go out on your own.

DO IT!

Like toddlers not venturing too far from their parents, you should keep a coach or mentor close by. These people will rotate out and help you level up as you move through your business. They should. You will have different needs, and you need to find the right ones for that part of your journey. Many times, you will hear this called, Leveling Up. And THAT is something you want to be continually working on.

Explore and put to practice all the experiences we have been taking in. So many people want to stay stuck in the learning phase and forget that to learn to speak, they had to put it into practice and SPEAK!

We may begin by starting dozens of songs on our own. By brainstorming and starting all sorts of creative projects and crossing the lines of as many genres as we feel we can enter. As we create ideas, we may even pass them off to others.

Remember that notebook you are carrying everywhere? Or maybe you've gravitated to a notes app on your device? Keep some pages in there that are just brainstorms you can bring to writing sessions. I will go as far as to sort them out, noting which writing session I will bring them to.

As you begin writing and collaborating with more people, you'll find each connection and collaboration fleshes out its own identity.

This allows you an opportunity to create your own thoughts on the themes and ideas that you bring to those specific projects or sessions.

Ultimately, we get to that run, and we are off to the races, looking for every and any opportunity to connect with other writers and creators, sharing ideas and manifesting new ones through those newly discovered partnerships.

It will feel as though things "seem" to be moving faster, and you could run out on your own.

Pick up a book daily and compound that personal development. In the fall of 2021, while diving hard into the mental toughness program 75 Hard, I read over 10 books, listened to five audiobooks and dozens of business and entrepreneur podcasts. Yes, there is a physical fitness part to the program; however, don't you think my brain muscle received the biggest workout during that time?

Case in point, you are reading this book or listening to the audiobook version, both of which are the results of that program being a mental catalyst in my creative journey. If you need a sneak peek or are just impatient, open Google and type in "75 Hard mental toughness program." That should keep you busy for a few moments—and most likely make your brain hurt a bit.

Abraham Lincoln stated: *"Give me six hours to chop down a tree, and I will spend the next four hours sharpening the axe."*

This process of constant professional development and sharpening your brain (axe), and increasing your quality of tools in the toolbox enhances and gives greater momentum to the growth inside your creative journey.

Many basketball players use "visual practice" to work on free throws. Proving to be one of the most nerve-racking parts of the game, they practice this over and over in their minds. Many of them say the likelihood of them making a free throw after this mental practice is 20-30% higher than not practicing it. This isn't to say that they don't spend hours and thousands of repetitions at the free-throw line. But they need to also have that visualization piece to complete the mind and body connection. They repeat the same process, routine, and form over and over till it is like breathing for them.

The hope is that this book, even if it's not the first part of your personal development journey, is the launching point somewhere in a long line of them to come!

Remember, as I said…

Do yourself a favor; each time you finish a book, sign the last page and date. EACH time you read it. YES, I said each time. Each time you read a book to grow your mind, YOU are a different person, and so a new version of you is reading it and receiving, interpreting, gathering, and putting into action different nuggets from the book.

I'm including a section in the back of the book as some starting points and resources for reading that pertain directly to the music industry. Though I most certainly have expanded my reading palette beyond just music as the subject, it's a great place to start.

If you want to know which book I'm reading right now, send a text message to me at 320-420-2105 using #ROADTO99READ, and I'll let you know!

INSIDER TIP

The average American reads about 12 books per year. Just think what you could do if you committed to reading two books per month instead of just one. You'd double the average!

CHAPTER 11

BE A GOOD HANG

"Waste no more time arguing what a good man should be.
Be one."
—Marcus Aurelius

So often, we walk down our journey and focus on our careers, believing that having better schooling, practicing longer hours, and alienating family and friends is "the way" to get that big gig, next promotion, or level up. Although those are certainly all components to being prepared for when those opportunities arrive, there is something even more important, especially in a relationship-based business. Just be a good hang!

I began my career as a sideman behind the drums with the Sweet Papa Dave blues band and then made a swift move to the country music scene. A few years into being in that scene, I wanted to further study the genre, the language, and how drummers and musicians were approaching the songs.

As I have done before, I started to seek out those who were at the top of the touring and recording list to ask just those questions. I began with Rich Redmond, who plays and records for country music artist Jason Aldean. This happened at the end of a clinic at the Percussive Arts Society International Convention (PASIC). I said a quick "hello," introduced myself, and asked a non-invasive question: "Can I reach out to you at a future date and ask you some questions about drumming in the country world?"

A second chance meeting was at a local bar that evening. For those of you who know the business world, THIS is often where business takes place. And by meeting, I mean just hanging out at the local bar with dozens of other drummers. How many conferences have you attended? The after-conference time at local hangs is where you will find attendees and where connections are made that you couldn't have dreamed of. After an event I attended in Dallas, TX, in early May of 2021, we had such a good hang that a quad shot of espresso was in my coffee the next morning.

While I was there with some friends, I made one more small connection. It started with some conversation that stemmed from an acknowledgment and thank you for a great clinic. I then let him know that I was looking forward to our future conversations. I left it at that. Walked away and just enjoyed the rest of the evening with my friends.

Recently while I was out on the road with the Shane Martin Band, I was chatting with some of the band members about the key component of having the best opportunities and being successful in pushing yourself to higher levels in the business. I'm going to give you the secret right here.

DON'T BE A JERK!

You need to be a good communicator while on stage performing, setting up, loading in gear, and on long bus and truck rides. On those long hotel days, when you have a gig that is a two-nighter, you have to be a good hang. Don't be a jerk.

The music business really boils down to being the people business.

Whether that is your bandmates, the venues that are hiring you, or the audience, you are there to entertain.

Ever been to a local coffee shop, bar, or favorite restaurant in the middle of the day or around 6 pm? There are all sorts of business deals taking place that you are grossly unaware of. Notice that these conversations are taking place where people can just hang out.

Be cool.
Be chill.
Be YOU.

A few weeks later, I reached out to Rich and said, "THANK YOU for the opportunity to chat," and just left the conversation open. I found out a few months later that Jason Aldean's tour would be coming through Minneapolis. I contacted Rich and offered to facilitate booking some private lessons for him to give while in town and help him with any travel needs he might have. He agreed to let me schedule some lessons for him. I quickly filled all the spots, and we were off and running!

By off and running, I mean, I had six spots filled for Rich to teach lessons, a practice room in the legendary Ellis Drum Shop in St. Paul, MN, a route to pick him up to grab a coffee to get the day going, and then hang out while he gave lessons to all those excited drummers. Drummers had the chance to take a lesson, get some consultation on the music industry, and one took the time to talk about his book and get some publishing advice. This played out well for that individual since Rich had recently released his book *CRASH! Course for Success: 5 Ways to Supercharge your Personal and Professional Life,* so publishing and launching a book was fresh in his mind.

The win for me was a day to hang with Rich in Minneapolis and to meet some more drummers from MN who wanted to fill those lesson spots. LOTS of conversations, questions, and thoughts about the music business ensued. I had an amazing time gaining insight, experiencing, getting a glimpse inside the touring world, and establishing a new relationship in the business.

I got a tour of the staging area for all the production equipment, the tour buses (I didn't get to go on them), and a trip around the actual stage they would be playing on that evening. Our time ended together by him treating me to lunch in the catering room. What a blast and a blessing! I even learned a few tricks about what food is good for fueling the body before playing a high-energy show. HINT: Not too many carbs right before you play. You'll lose large amounts of energy and be a bit lethargic.

Xcel Energy Center in St. Paul, MN, from the set of Jason Aldean's show.

I was surprised where our conversation headed next. He said, "Jeremy, if you want to continue learning, connect with my other two friends who travel the country road just like me. You need to take a lesson with Garrett and Jim." I was on it for sure!

I first reached out to Garrett and got something scheduled for a lesson and started working with him. We sat and chatted about business coaching for advancing my drumming career from a regional artist in the Midwest to a larger scale touring artist. Forty-five minutes into our conversation, he just stopped and said, "Jeremy, you can do this. Just get down here, and let's get you meeting people."

WOW! I felt like that just completely came out of leftfield.

If there has ever been a moment in a lesson or coaching session that I have been in that could be considered a "mic drop" moment, that was it.

From there forward, he helped me set up a few meetings and taught me how to strategize on making multiple trips to Nashville every year to appear "in town" and be available for any potential gig coming up. These meetings were with his contacts and connections in Nashville. Remember earlier when I talked about ending up on Nate's one-bedroom apartment couch? Well, here's how that played out.

Hanging with Garrett Goodwin after the
Carrie Underwood concert in Minneapolis, MN.

When someone is letting me into their circle of influence and connecting me with their folks, I take it quite seriously and guard it with my life. In this case, it wasn't from a standpoint that I thought I'd "screw it up," but that I wanted to make sure I provided the right follow-through and brought my A-game to every meeting.

What I was soon to find out was all that I really had to do was keep on being the best version of myself. That's what lead me to even have these conversations, meetings, and opportunities in the first place.

After a few months of phone calls, dozens of emails, and text messages, I was on a plane. All my meetings were set up, and I was ready to tackle them head-on! The first one was an amazing visit and hang during a session at Yellowhammer Studios in East Nashville. Top-notch studio, gear, setup, and an even better hang. That first late-night recording session in Nashville with some incredible people was only the beginning of that trip.

I had the opportunity to watch the process happen right before my eyes, all while just having good conversation and lots of laughs with the other musicians. If you get a chance, check out Jada Vance on Spotify, a fun-spirited country artist who has some super cool stuff happening!

**Yes, it seems like some shameless promotion,
but this is the music business, and everyone deserves
a chance to be heard and share their art with the world.**

Therefore, you've already encountered some opportunities to discover some new music through these pages.

Night number two was even more of a wild ride! A friend of mine who I've known since college and who had been already living and working in Nashville for about seven years worked the "Broadway scene" quite heavily. This is the section in downtown Nashville where the most tourist-driven bars are located.

If you don't know what I'm referring to, it is sometimes called "Nash Vegas." Late nights, bright lights, and LOTS of live music. Many of the venues have two or three floors of bars, and each floor has a different band playing, and they all switch up every four hours. What you should also know is that these bands don't take set breaks like you might experience at other venues across the US. So, these musicians are working the music scene hard. They might even work double and triple shifts some days.

That evening he took me into almost every bar, whether the venue had one floor or three, and introduced me to the bands and any musician who may have just been hanging out. He even threw me up on stage to play a few songs with one of the bands.

Even though that trip was just the first…it was the beginning of returning to Nashville every six to eight weeks, per the suggestion of Garrett, to continue building and nurturing those relationships. Even five years later, I stop and visit those musicians from that very first band I sat in with.

INSIDER TIP

Meet people. Provide value. Give back.
And most important:
BE A GOOD HANG!

RECORD & RELEASE

CHAPTER 12

BUILDING THE TEAM

"If you want to go fast, go alone.
If you want to go far, go together."
—African Proverb

Over the past few years, through all the trips to Nashville, Dallas, Austin, Los Angeles, Santa Monica, and San Diego, I have been building my team. I'm getting the right musicians I trust and who are the best at what they do. Just because your neighbor, family member, or high school friend plays guitar doesn't mean they can function in a high-pressure studio session. Fast decisions need to be made. In mere moments, they need to come up with a whole new version of what they just did.

These are the types of musicians, writers, and engineers that I have worked at surrounding myself with. It helps me push the creative elements of the song and bring something to the artist that is far beyond what they could've conceived as they begin to put lyrics and melody to paper.

Neuroscientist Oliver Sacks states: *"More than 50% of the known mapped parts of the brain are stimulated while listening to music. This increases, even more, when a musician is playing an instrument or creating the music they are listening to."*

When I hear a scientist speak about music like this, when it's under the most scrutinized research conditions, it pushes me to create something even greater every time. To learn something new each time.

I see how far I can push my writing partners as well as the musicians and engineers we are using to produce the song.

I'm always gaining new knowledge about myself, the creative process, the artists I'm working with, AND the audience that consumes these songs once they hit the streaming services and airwaves.

It ALWAYS turns out in the direction we are headed, but NEVER the way we thought it would.

Bringing a song together under the right conditions: the musicians, the writers, the recording space, the instruments—and little divine inspirations—will always yield a result that the people in the room couldn't have thought of before they entered.

When working with My Corner Retreat on their song "Free Fall," our beginning conversations were around creating a sonorous and floating lullaby that the listener could just sonically fall into. As I began building the track and adding drums, bass, and guitar, it transformed into the perfect combination of Marvin Gaye, Stevie Wonder, and Bill Withers. Much to the client's delight, the song hit even harder on their emotional strings and elevated the vocal performance that landed on the track. Check out My Corner Retreat's website on the Resources page to listen to a few more songs from that collaboration.

The second release from The Dumpsterfire was a song titled "Nights Like These." This song began as lyrically dark and ominous. We were worried it was a bit too dark to even work on as a releasable song as it might create too much angst. As we began recording and putting the pieces together, it turned into more of a celebration of moving forward and enjoying the moment.

Take a listen and hear it for yourself. We'd love to know your thoughts! Refer to the website link for The Dumpsterfire on the *Resources* page at the beginning of the book.

I recently finished another song with My Corner Retreat out of Chicago and their song "Atmospheric Conditions" is the perfect representation of this idea. Musicians from three different cities tracked parts of the song. None of the parts were created in the same space. The unifying factors were finding the right players, discussing, discovering the true meaning behind the lyrics, and then getting out of the way and letting everyone do their part.

Of course, there are edits, tweaks, and small changes as you move closer to the final product. However, everyone has the same goal of serving the song in the best way possible. There were actually a few cases on this one where people had to re-record their entire parts because they wanted to serve the song at a deeper level.

One rule I have for myself when producing an artist and their songs, and even more so when we are talking about the songs where I am part of the writing process, is finding the right players for each part, for each song. Yes, that means sometimes we use multiple players for the instruments based on which song is next.

Through countless hours of conversations and meetings, I've built this amazing team. Many times they don't even know that they were collaborating with each other. I love that this is the case most of the time for clients in my studio.

However, I am finding out through multiple people that there are conversations being had about the process I'm using, and they are always curious about what I will be sending them next.

For the record, this isn't the only way that I work the process. I also hire session players and bring everyone into the studio at one time and build the track. This is the more traditional way the process works, and it sure has its benefits from an efficiency and creativity standpoint. However, sometimes for the client, it isn't geographically possible. I am constantly trying to come up with ways to break down the barriers musicians have in recording and releasing their own music.

Empty Page Studios, my studio, was built and developed with this idea in mind.

Bring together musicians from across the world to make music and make an impact in the industry.

Here's a suggestion when putting a team together.

Treat them well.

Pay them well.

Keep on hiring them!!

Soon they will be connecting with you and asking when the next project is going to land in their inbox. These are the people you want around you all the time. The more times that you share in the creative process, the further you will push each other, as well. Iron sharpens iron, and so, everyone can raise their level of creativity and sonically bring it all together.

When you are working with a great team, the synergy you create is beyond measurable. Brendan stated that he was surprised at my ability to be a songwriting chameleon from one project to the next.

Finding the right people and putting them in the right places, letting them do what they do best, means not only will they shine, but it gives you the opportunity to let the things you do come shining to the front.

My old store manager at Office Depot used to tell me, "You have to put your aces in their places." That's exactly what I work so hard on every project.

INSIDER TIP

Take as many opportunities to work with others as possible. Allow your team to rise to the top and form into alignment. This is synergy hard at work.

CHAPTER 13

FINISH THE DAMN THING

"If you hear a certain sound in your head, you should never settle for less than that. You should find that exact sound."
—James Rotondi, Producer for Post Malone

The creation and recording process in music is one of searching, developing, creating, crafting, manipulation, disagreement, and growth. Well, if just reading those seven words didn't make you want to stop your recording process or creative journey, please keep reading. We will get through this.

The world is full of starters, workers, and finishers. Which one are you?

There are many ways to approach the recording process, but for the purposes of our conversation here, it will be started and, yes, finished by you.

There will be excuses, roadblocks, COVID-19 (at this point, it is still a thing). Just last week, I had a full four-day recording session with my co-writer to produce four new songs. We had two studios booked, engineers scheduled, guitar players, bass players, saxophonists, flights, hotels, cars all scheduled. Twenty-six hours before the first flight, someone got COVID-19.

Yep, *ALL canceled.* Well, I'm sure that's what your brain thought right away. Mine went in a different direction. I chose to take the view that it was postponed. Reframe that moment and just give it a different name. Within the rest of my 45-minute drive to a rehearsal, I had all the flights, cars, and accommodations canceled or postponed, and all the players were notified.

For the players' sake, I wanted to make sure they had the opportunity to fill that time with other sessions and work. Here's one large difference in how I run my studio and, as a producer, work within the music community. I respect people's time. I pay them more—as much as the artist budget will allow. And I hire them as much as I can. I respect their talents. They have earned it. And many of these players I had booked at least six to eight weeks prior to those sessions. So, filling those time slots for them was essential.

Research tells us that less than 5% of the population never experience *musical frisson* or the idea of getting "goosebumps" when they hear a piece of music. Can you imagine?

It's almost like saying they don't have a heartbeat, which we know not to be true, at least if they are standing and conversing with you. When I tell people this during a workshop or training, they are dumbfounded. Many find it quite unbelievable.

So, pushing yourself, the artist, and the players to go beyond just mediocre is essential. Take the simplest idea and transform it into a sonic journey for the listener. Some producers and artists parallel this to going with your gut. In the digital recording world we live in today, there are so many opportunities to just keep stacking, and stacking, and stacking without actually standing back and listening to what's going on.

In simple terms:

K – eep
I – t
S – imple
S – illy

The recording process is much like putting together a 4D puzzle. We begin with the essential three parts: the lyrics, the instrumentals, and the players. The fourth is most definitely where the magic happens. Then we put all of those into perfect alignment with rhythm, melody, and harmony.

The Dumpsterfire at Sound Kitchen Studios.

INSIDER TIP

The double bar IS your best friend.
Good and done is better than something left unfinished.

CHAPTER 14

RELEASING IT!

"Creativity is intelligence having fun."
–Albert Einstein

Don't they want people to hear it?? Repeatedly this is the part that many musicians seem to gloss over. I mean, they just spent thousands of dollars and hundreds of hours of time getting this music written, recorded, and mixed.

Sometimes it is fear or even imposter syndrome setting in. They think, *why would anyone want to listen to this? Will anyone outside my family and friends even like it? What value am I bringing to the listener by releasing it?*

NONE of that matters!!

What matters is that you created a piece of art that you were inspired to make with others.

In that process, others were inspired to create the best parts possible to support that.

These first two songs got softly released with a couple of lyric videos, and a few people even liked them.

Check them out here:

"Everyday" bit.ly/dfeveryday

"High Ball" bit.ly/dfhighball

Or don't check them out. That's totally okay, too. Again, it doesn't matter! Some people will, and some won't. That's great! Because some WILL!

When Mark and I are releasing music, which we do monthly, sometimes I forget which song we are on. I have since started marking the name of the song on the release date on my calendar. We are usually finishing a song and getting it into the distribution channels six to eight weeks before the actual release date.

Mark and I like to call this looking for a unicorn. Mostly because there are tens of thousands of songs being released every day, so you are just hoping you are the unicorn. And if not, there is always next month. Some of you have a version of this about your favorite sports team, "Well, there is always next year." The important thing is that we keep on releasing songs month after month. I started writing the book in November of 2021; we are now in March of 2022, and we have recorded songs that are ready to release through May 2022.

This is what the process can look like. We like it because we are constantly staying ahead. Since Mark and I work in sync licensing, music in TV, and the film space as well, we can tackle small one-off projects or special requests in a quick and timely manner. This is because we have our regular release schedule so far out. Sync licensing provides a unique opportunity in songwriting to work on themes and genres you might not "normally" think of.

You need to choose your lyrics in a manner that paints a story without getting too specific. Remember, the audio in TV and film is there to support and enhance the visual story. The challenge is making sure you feel satisfied as an artist and creator while fitting it to the visual components!

My planning is constantly in motion, and always looking three to six months out. It keeps things moving forward and your calendar full and planned. So when hiccups occur, you hit a roadblock, or something happens where you need to take a personal break, business doesn't just stop.

A huge benefit for you is that it gives you an opportunity to take a break. The beauty of working for yourself is you get to make the schedule, the timelines, and the vacations. You certainly need to be careful in this space as you don't want to vacation your business away.

What if you plan your recording and writing sessions around your vacations and self-care moments?

I do it both ways. Many times, I know that I need to travel for a recording session, training, conference, or writing session. Why not add a few more days onto the trip and enjoy some self-care and vacation time? Take this time to give your mental state of mind some respite. Remember, we read earlier that music consumes at least 50% of the brain. Well, if you are running at a constant rate, that brain, which is a muscle, does need some recovery time.

Getting the music just right in those final stages before releasing it is essential. Nate and I have had the distinct pleasure of working with Brendan Ruane as a mix engineer whose experience and ears bring a fantastic combination of modern and vintage sound.

Valuing what the listeners think, feel, and experience when they experience your music is a top priority for me. It is that emotional connection to music, the goosebumps—also called musical frisson—that lets you know the song captured a truly magical experience.

It is essential for those moments to happen more often as you are writing and recording. The more times that you can hit that mark, the more often you are going to capture larger and larger audiences. This helps lead to them sharing it!

INSIDER TIP

If you get your song into the streaming platforms at least four to six weeks early, you have the opportunity for playlist curators to take a listen and possibly add it to their list.

REFLECT

CHAPTER 15

LET'S TALK ABOUT IT

"We are what we repeatedly do.
Excellence then is not an act, but a habit."
—Aristotle

Each process along the way is one where we need to stop, process, reflect, and learn from the process that has just taken place. The military calls these after-action reports or AARs. And they take these VERY seriously as they affect the lives of their fellow soldiers and civilians. Though we are on the glorious and sometimes treacherous Road to 99, at a few points and certainly once we finish each small process, there needs to be a space for reflection on the events and process that just took place.

After each song, we take the time to stop and reflect on what happened during that session. Not that we sit with a sheet of paper and a list of questions; however, we keep a few of the below thoughts in the back of our minds as we are in conversation.

DID WE GET FASTER?

Fast just simply means, did we achieve an increased level of efficiency with this song than we had in the past? This isn't to say we are working on a speed timeline. The goal isn't to see "how fast" we can finish a song. But there are days we get stuck on one lyric line for 15-20 minutes. We get hung up.

We continually remind ourselves to move on. We can come back to it. It's in those moments that you need to give yourself the opportunity to find a new line later. Here's a secret: something later will most definitely inspire what needs to be put into that spot.

We never ask these questions or have these conversations out of negativity. It should be the process at the end of each session that makes the next one go even better! AND, it doesn't even have to be with that person. You bring that criticism and positive feedback into every session going forward.

When you begin a new writing session, whether it's with someone you have written with many times or you are writing with someone for the first time, you have to slow down to speed up.

My wife, to this day, still calls these mini therapy sessions. It would be quite convenient if I could start billing insurance companies for writing and recording sessions. Who knows, maybe this book is the beginning of those conversations and working with those businesses. New funding sources for the studio. Now that is some creative thinking!

It's the reconnection of what was lost from the week before. What has been gained since we last spoke? This is a connection between two musicians and two individuals coming from two different worlds and spaces. So often, if it's been more than a week, we can have these conversations and still keep them short. We still have work to do and the task to complete. We don't waste that time for sure.

Sometimes it's a needed moment to work through an issue one of you may have had in the past few days. Compartmentalizing your thoughts and differentiating from your daily headaches isn't always easy to do. The "check your shit at the door" mentality doesn't always work. So, let's just get that shit out on the table and not allow it to be a barrier.

Now we can create. Now the ideas can flow. Or, at the very least, we can create the space it needs to happen.

Human beings are daily looking, longing, and seeking these types of connections. So why would it seem odd or out of character for two individuals, musicians, artists, or creators, to need to dive into that?

As often as we think we should do this, I actually believe this is quite mandatory for co-writing and collaboration. It seems those moments of what appears like a brief conversation are what truly bring the songs and music to life.

Recently I had a writing session scheduled with a co-writer I hadn't seen in a while. We just spent the two-hour session talking about life, business, music, and moving forward. We both had to laugh at the end of the session, as we hadn't written a single lyric or melody. The joke was, "There was a hit song in that conversation somewhere. I guess we'll just have to find out next time." We booked the next writing session right away.

INSIDER TIP

If a writing session goes well,
BOOK THE NEXT ONE!
Why wait?!

CHAPTER 16

LEARN FROM EACH OTHER

"I learned that losing is no more than an action, lesson learned, or mistake that requires you to analyze and adjust and sometimes apologize."
—#TooStrong: How to Win Fast and Win Often in a World Full of Obstacles, Mike Claudio

Venting…sometimes one of us just needs a moment to get things off our chest. It usually has nothing to do with any of the other people in the room. It has been said so many times that a writing room or a creative collaboration is much like a group therapy circle. Whether it is just a moment to help clear someone's head or open an opportunity to clear some air in the room, it's deep inside these conversations and clearings that we find small tidbits of ideas.

There are whispers of words and themes looming in the air.

An idea of "word riffing" came from working with a Minnesota country and metal rock artist, Mark Stone. This isn't necessarily a conversation but an opportunity to throw out ideas. They are also called Brain Showers—as I mentioned earlier. But let's face it, word riffing is way cooler to talk about in a book. For the record, that's not a typo. Mark *really does* do country and heavy metal. He has the perfect voice to do those 80's rock and heavy metal lyrics and then step up to the microphone and sing a subtle country song.

So we let the ideas just flow, then search for those themes and similar phrases to arise. This riffing leads to dozens of ideas and filling pages and pages of notebook paper as we flesh out digital characters. Then we sift through them later to see if there is something of substance that we both gravitate to. As we do, we continually stay open to what others have to say.

Here's where you need to double down.

Listen.

Then listen.

Then listen some more.

God gave you two ears and one mouth for a reason.

Listen to what the other person is contributing, internalize it, and then send something back their way. I'm not saying that you should shut yourself down. Or feel like you can't contribute. You should stick your neck out there.

Which parts make it challenging yet still so fulfilling and rewarding as a creator?

It's this constant process of reflection that seems to feed and bring even more fuel to the next writing session. It's as though our ideas and plans and delusions of grandeur have become the thoughts we put by the wayside, and the process and journey are the things that we continue to embrace. Hold tightly. Guard your time and thoughts. They are the most valuable thing you have.

Yet even in doing this, we respect the time we have. Don't take more. Don't waste the small windows in your week. Well, yes, of course, there is a conversation, catch-up, banter, and discussion, but we know what we showed up for, and we are most certainly going to make that happen.

Learning from each other is essential. It's not just about the music or process, but about life. Everyone has an amazing story to offer, and inside that story are dozens of golden nuggets you can bring into your life.

INSIDER TIP

YOU are the only one who has your story. Share it with others, as it will inspire them. Even though they may never even tell you.

REPEAT

CHAPTER 17

DON'T STOP THERE

"Write...submit...forget...repeat!"
-TAXI Music Licensing Owner

Time and time again, I hear from people in the music industry, visual arts, and book publishers that they just wrote a song or a book, or even a masterpiece on their canvas. All those are amazing and sometimes even monumental things in an artist's career. Yet, the comment and response from management staff, agencies, record labels, and ultimately consumers is: "Fantastic! What else do you have?"

It appears we forget that just because we did one or even a few, or many love the "product," we still need to continue to create the next painting, sculpture, book, or song. *Can you do it again?* Some people spend the rest of their lives trying to write their second number one song, forgetting that all they did to write the first one was to keep repeating their process and doing the work until they found one that someone decided was worthy of pushing to the top.

Just so you know, to date, I have not had a song go to number one on the charts, but trust me, I'm not stopping till I get there. So, I just keep that process going and do the work!

It's not just a product, song, or canvas we have to keep repeating. We need to continue the process of working with new collaborations. To repeat something literally means to "keep repeating it." You may choose to adjust the approach and process of how those interactions take place but repeat them, nonetheless. And you can learn something from every one of them.

What is it about your approach?

What are you bringing to the table?

In what ways are you reacting positively and negatively to what the other person across the room, table, or computer screen is adding to the collaboration?

CJ WILDER

CJ is my brother in musical arms, a bass player, and an amazing music producer. He was ONE of the amazing people I met on that first night in Nashville. He is a humble, unassuming, amazing musician, human being, and bass player. Shortly after we "met," I remembered in a flash that we had truly met a year prior, at a show we shared the bill on in Las Vegas during the National Finals Rodeo. It seemed like an even smaller world at that moment. Yet, this would not be the last time we would cross paths.

A couple of trips later, once Nate and I had finished writing a few songs, we decided to take them into the studio and experience the creative process through a producer and creator lens. The first full day and late into the night—3:00 am to be exact—we tracked and recorded the foundation of two songs. We had to get them ready; the guitar player, pedal steel player, and bass player were all coming the next day in shifts to fill in the rest of the parts.

Well, the first one who was supposed to show was the bass player, my friend from college...no call, no show, no way to get a hold of him. What were we supposed to do at that point? Other players were coming in the rest of the day and the next morning. I made a quick call to CJ, who was a referral from another friend. I mean, how else was I going to get a number to connect? He was there within 45 minutes, and we hit the ground running! He, of course, knocked those bass parts out of the park and provided the perfect pairing with my drums to solidify the rhythm backbone of both songs.

Just a few short months later, CJ and I met again, and this time solidified the beginning of a long-standing musical relationship and even better friendship! It was from that point forward that CJ became the bass player who I always hired when producing tracks for artists coming through my studio. Even if I needed a demo or something for my own songs, he was always the one I called.

His keen sense for sound, the song, and helping me bring the right players together was amazing. I took so many of those thoughts, conversations, and approaches forward as I continued to grow the list of artists and co-writers I worked with.

As I fast forward to a couple of years later, after dozens of times working together, meeting for coffee when I was in town, and going for runs as the weather permitted, we found ourselves working on writing some songs together. As we sat and worked on our second one, we began talking about our dads—who, come to find out—we both lost at a similar point of time in our lives.

It became about memories and reminiscing on what our individual experiences were with our dads. To this date, this is the fastest song I've ever co-written with someone. It was as though the lyrics couldn't flow onto the paper fast enough.

We quickly ran into his house and grabbed his wife to sit and listen to make sure what we were saying was not just sappy nonsense. All three of us had tears leaking from our eyes as we finished that first "performance" of the song for her. It certainly felt like we hit the mark on that one!

I can proudly say that we finally got that song recorded after four years and released it. In the interest of a good shameless musician plug, go check out "You're There" on iTunes, buy it, and add the streaming link to the playlist you put on repeat.

I take that back. I PROUDLY share that with you and don't even feel bad about it. It's what we are supposed to be doing. If you have put that much time into writing, editing, reworking, demoing, tracking, mixing, creating artwork, getting set up on all your channels, and finally releasing it, then proclaim it loudly and share often!

Here's a quick exercise…

List five people or memories you could write about right now:

1. ______________________________
2. ______________________________
3. ______________________________
4. ______________________________
5. ______________________________

INSIDER TIP

You will be surprised how those memories will inspire a lyric, a melody, or an emotion that will send you down a path to something quite special.

CHAPTER 18

CREATIVE BLOCKS

"Having a healthy body, creating a strong mind, and a successful life are built on repetition. And 95% of these activities aren't the most glamorous either."
—Kris Whitehead, Becoming Iconic

Nothing replaces time. Time spent in practice. Time spent learning your craft. Getting criticism and feedback from coaches. Time spent doing the work. Putting new strategies into action.

Do the work.

Write over and over. Work toward the opportunity to find those who are ready to record and release. Then work through conversations with your co-writers and collaborators to figure out what worked and where you can improve next time.

It's so important to just finish it. My composition professor in college used to constantly remind me to "put a double bar" down and move on.

For those of you who might not know, that is the final bar line for a song or composition. He continued to tell me that you learned what you needed to from this one. Now move on. Each song, each writing session, each recording session, each release, and every interaction afterward ignites an opportunity to learn something new and put it into practice and action for the next time around.

Here I am talking about the work. Talking about the action. Let me give you some questions that we kept in mind throughout the process, and as we were growing, that can many times lead to slowing your process. Or, as I like to call it, paralysis by analysis. All too often, this can stop the creative process dead in its tracks. So, let's tackle a few of those creative blocks!

WHAT'S A "GOOD" SONG?

This is a long-sought-after and elusive question that only the masses might be able to answer. I mean, they are the ones who allow it to rise to that level—that and a few hundred thousand dollars from records companies, advertisers, and radio station collaborations.

Even then, it bears the question as to whether it is a "good song."

Dare I say a good song is in the ears of the beholder or listener. Although there may be some formulas and "genetic" design to good songs by writers whose songs seem to rise to the top time and time again, it still boils down to those listener requests on the radio and their playlists being filled with those songs on repeat.

So many times, as songwriters and producers, I find that groups of people talk about what is "right" for a song as being synonymous with what is "good."

What is right for the song are the pieces of sonic layers and opportunities we are inspired to include in the moment of creation. Those moments of spontaneous creation are some of the most magical times we have in the recording and creation process. There are even times when mistakes are made after dozens of takes on a track.

**We call those moments happy mistakes,
and we sometimes leave them in there,
as they add character and value for the listener.**

I'll even go as far as to leave small snippets of sonic elements in a track, tucked away in the back and down low in the mix, just to see how deeply the listener is listening. Trust me. These are moments you most likely won't hear when you are listening in the car or on a pair of cheap headphones. However, for the audiophiles, those people who listen to the most finite details of a song, and folks who want to dive deeper into a song, and its buried sonic textures, I've most certainly hidden things in every track! Happy hunting!

Other times these conversations lead to heated debates between friends and fellow creators. A good friend of mine once told me as I was starting to build my studio and client base, "No good music was ever made without disagreement and discussion." That statement still resonates loudly with me today.

I think there is another lesson inside there. You need to be able to work through those tough moments in the studio. Yes, there will be moments when you need to make split-second decisions, and though it might not be the majority rule, you have to run with it. "Someone" has to be the final decision guy. However, there is also the part that you need to work on until it's right.

Recently I was working with a client in Texas, and the session was cruising right along. Then we came to a song that continued to present roadblock after roadblock. I came up with all sorts of alternatives and ways to work through the pain spots and ended up feeling like we were forcing something that just wasn't ready. I stopped the session and said, "We are moving on and will just need the whole song to be reworked before we can come back to it." This brought a sigh of relief to everyone in the session.

Being a producer and the one managing people, emotions, music, gear, and egos in a high-pressure environment pushes you to a whole new level of self and situational awareness. All those pieces on their own are a challenge but put them together, and it is a delicate melting pot you need to manage. The explosion can be something you can never return from, OR it can be some of the most magical music you could ever create!

After hundreds of conversations and my own study and research, I've found there are two pieces that make up a good song. The writer and creators are in love with it. And when shared with an audience, it can connect with the listener over and over.

Connecting with a listener can be done with any number of attributes of a song. It could be the melody and the flow. They might love the beat and the groove because of the way it makes them move, dance, or feel. The lyrics and the message it sends may resonate with them based on a past event or shared experience. Those are four big-picture or macro ideas that can draw a listener into a song. Capturing a listener in all four domains is a sure-fire way to make sure they will become an evangelist for your song.

All musicians start with the same 12 notes.

The same set of rhythmic attributes is based on basic music theory guidelines. Therefore, we are all creating remixes of combinations that have already been worked with. I constantly find myself repeating this, "Bach screwed it up for everyone because everything written after him is just some version of it."

With ONE difference.

YOU!

Insert YOU into that equation and all those notes, lyrics, rules, tempos, etc., and the sonic palette becomes a whole new playground. You are one in six billion. This makes you the single most creative and unique version of YOU. Sure, this sounds redundant. If we know we are created as unique individuals, then why do we spend so much of our time attempting to conform?

DO PEOPLE REALLY WRITE ABOUT THAT?

As you begin to build a library of songs, adding more co-writing and collaboration opportunities to your weekly schedule, you'll find that the subject matter of your songs will also continue to expand and evolve.

Creating daily means you will HAVE to continue diving deeper into any subject matter you choose. You may at times even find yourself writing about things that may be uncomfortable to you.

Get comfortable with being uncomfortable. It's essential to the creative process and becoming the best version of yourself. I have read page after page of business books that profile successful entrepreneurs, business owners, and companies. One theme that returns time and time again is living outside your comfort zone.

If we are living in that fuzzy, warm, sitting-by-a-fireplace-where-everything-is-an-easy-sort-of-life space, we are not allowing opportunities for friction, error, mistakes, strife, and challenges. It's in these spaces where you can grow the most and push yourself even further beyond what your current version looks like.

In August of 2021, I started day one of a program called 75 Hard. As I began the program, most people thought I was nuts. In hindsight, in the beginning, I probably was a little crazy. Yet, so often, as we enter into the music business, family and friends think we are quite crazy, as well.

However, in my personal and business life, I was looking for something to change. I needed a direction and avenue that would catapult me into high gear and provide a rocket-fueled push into the future. Let me tell you, THIS was IT! But it did take me until day 50 to see the transformational benefits as well as how far-reaching the program was into my mind, life, and business.

In the weeks before I started, I read the book *75 Hard* by Andy Frisella, the mastermind and creator of the 75 Hard program. THIS was when my mindset changed about whether I "thought" I could do it.

The book methodically laid out the philosophy behind the program, and more to my liking, it spelled out what the brain and body were going to experience throughout the various stages of days. It's quite like how our mindset and process changed, developed, and transformed as Nate and I worked through our songwriting journey from Song 1 to Song 68.

The challenge is far more than just a "fitness program" that many folks perceive it to be. It's a mental toughness program. It's doing simple tasks daily for 75 days straight.

- No changes.
- No manipulations.
- No compromises.
- No making it fit your day or mind.
- If you have to ask, the answer is no.

Therein lies the mental toughness. In music, in songwriting, in creating, we LIVE in a space of needing mental toughness beyond even our own belief.

I was also super fortunate that only two days into starting the program, a friend reached out to me and asked if I wanted to be a part of a Facebook Messenger group of business owners who were also starting 75 Hard. I, of course, said YES! There were many days that I wouldn't have made it through my tasks for the day without this group. For that, I am forever grateful for the "Savage 75 Hard" Facebook group.

The one thing I also noticed was how spot-on the book was. Even though we were all there to support each other, there were still times when people would have to start over—even if they'd made it all the way up to day seventy-five. All the markers where the book said it would be a challenge are when those drops happened. The awesome part was that everyone in the group was still there to support everyone. Regardless of what "day" we were on.

I'm not the only one who has done this. YOU aren't the only one who has ever journeyed down a creative path. Here are some paths that a few others have started and that they have fallen on along their way:

1. Writing a book
2. Painting a mural
3. Composing a symphony
4. Designing a new machine
5. Releasing industry-changing software
6. Drawing an architectural masterpiece
7. Creating an innovative workplace solution for teams

"Turn the quiet up; turn the noise down."
—Eric Church

Are you willing to turn the noise down? Stop listening to what others "say" you should do. Most times, these are the people who will spend years thinking about doing something but won't act on it. It's much easier for them to criticize you and tell you how you won't be able to accomplish what you want to do.

Recently I met some people who are a part of a mastermind group called APEX. They will support your thoughts, help you discover ideas, and push you to implement them. These are the people you want to spend your time with. I'm not saying you have to rid yourself of those other folks who might just be close friends, co-workers, or even family. However, limiting time and setting some boundaries is a fantastic way to make sure what you are working toward is the focus.

For over 20 years at family gatherings and events with friends, I am invariably asked a version of the same question, "Are you still doing that music thing?" Music thing!!! I've been working as a full-time musician for well over a decade and was building toward it before that. I'd say I'm still doing the "thing."

Although sometimes my "eye roll" tells a different story, I do welcome the question. It gives me an opportunity to talk about what I have been doing. Sometimes it's fun to even come up with more creative ways to talk about it. If you are in this position, you can word your response differently, play games with it, and have fun with it. It's what YOU do!! Even though I'm a drummer, producer, songwriter, speaker, coach, realtor—and now an author—at the end of the day, I'm truly a business owner!

Even then, you want to create opportunities to filter out some of those weird questions and awkward conversations. Although, I've never really understood why they are asked. Being a business owner, especially as it pertains to the music industry, is just not comprehensible to most people. The career paths of doctor, lawyer, accountant, or school teacher are better understood by most. As we've already stated, the path of a musician, business owner, or entrepreneur is not one that is just "laid out" for you.

The crazy part is, in this role, you are all these things:

1. Sales department
2. Marketing department
3. Accounting department
4. Legal department
5. Executive committee
6. Research and development
7. AND the CEO

I'd say there is a little more to it than just a "thing."

INSIDER TIP

"If people are doubting how far you can go, go so far that you can't hear them anymore."
—Michele Ruiz

CHAPTER 19

BUILDING THE BRIDGE

"There are some days when I think I'm going to die from an overdose of satisfaction."
—Salvador Dali

Would you want something cheap and easy for your children? What legacy do you want to leave for them? Would it be one of:

- Hard work
- Dedication
- Integrity
- Persistence
- Gratitude

Boy, when you use those words, it certainly changes how you think about it. I would hope that it also changes how quickly you are approaching it. Regardless of where we come from, the upbringing we've had, or our experiences that have led to where we are now, we ALL can agree on one thing. As parents, we always want the best for our children and their future.

I'm over here building a machine that will leave a legacy for my children, grandchildren, and great-grandchildren.

I'm changing the culture and family legacy trajectory. I 100% believe that I am making my dad, the angel on my shoulder, smile down on me and the direction my family is headed.

Let's face it, if you just read the last three paragraphs, I gave you some ideas and prompts for six songs you can bring to your next writing session. Dig deep and find them.

Digging deep and finding that inner fire and burning desire, motivation, and passion are essential as you begin, advance, and catapult forward in the music business. Well, let's not stop there.... This is applicable in every business when you are an entrepreneur or CEO. It's the motivation and inner fire that will get you going in the beginning, but it's the passion and the burning desire for what you know you were put here to do that will make those monumental shifts happen for you.

These shifts make it possible for you to move through the stress, hurdles, late nights, early mornings, hundreds of hours of research, and thousands of hours of typing and answering emails—of which many go unanswered or are just pushed away.

Here are a few phrases I have used dozens of times over the years and that I have now taught to my children. They use these all the time, and they will even send them back to me at times.

- *"Go ahead and build a bridge, so you can get over it."*
- *"You can either be frustrated or fascinated."*
- *"Early is on-time; on-time is late."*

Giving your children tools like this, even when you think they aren't listening, will manifest traits like positive thinking, perseverance, and hard work as they grow into adulthood. My oldest daughter has graduated, moved out, and is working full-time. Yes, I'm a proud father for sure! However, some of my favorite conversations take place when she returns for a family dinner and some laundry. That's when I hear her say things like, "Dad, I just told them to build a bridge," or "Wow, I was really fascinated when my co-workers were acting lazy and unproductive at work today."

Go ahead, take these examples, and put them into your phrase vocabulary. See how differently you think and can respond to a potentially challenging situation in your day.

INSIDER TIP

Bring your children into the mix of what you are doing musically. Show them what you are doing and talk about why you are doing it. Teaching them about following their dreams and that it takes hard work is just one of your tasks as an amazing parent.

NEW DIRECTION

CHAPTER 20
YOUR JOURNEY

"Music always makes me feel less alone in the mess."
—Brené Brown

An idea.
A process.
A journey.
A reflection.

The intent of this book was to give you a glimpse into my journey. One, yes one, version of what the Road to 99 can look like. Countless hours, meetings, gallons of coffee, Zoom meetings, late-night recording sessions, and more.

That was all stacked up with the purpose to write, record, and release music into the world—music that speaks to others and brings value to their musical soul.

The amazing, nerve-racking, and exciting part of building your business is that no two stores are alike. Embrace that! Millions of people own businesses, and all their stories are different. Remember the fact that we are one in six billion little swimmers that made it to their destination.

Will you embark on your journey?

Embrace the process?

Take time to understand each moment. Go inside your brain. Take it ALL in, every opportunity, every conversation, every chance meeting, every opportunity to show work and be heard.

The Road to 99 is most certainly not for everyone. That's okay! In fact, it's to our benefit!! If everyone were on the journey and walking that path, would there be room for all of them? How would we make it through the pack?

Plenty of people will try and talk you down, tell you it's not a great idea, and will wonder when you will ever get a real job. The sad part is that about 80% of people don't even like their job or what they do 40 hours a week. You don't have to be that person—especially since most of the people telling you "not to" are those eighty percent.

I'm not saying you should just up and quit your job and pivot on a moment's notice. I'm saying you should plan for it. Prepare for it.

Before I went "full-time" into running my music business, I was working full-time in a retail management position, in essence, working 70-80 hours a week. Trust me; I learned a lot in retail management. Working in a retail "box store" setting teaches you a ton about working with all types of customers. The nice part was that every day was just a little different.

This gave me opportunities to be creative in that space. I learned how to tackle challenges, inventory, and shipping issues, how to address employee tension and retention, as well as what went into firing employees and succession planning.

When you are working in a management position, employee management, inventory flow, district expectations, and corporate goals for your financials are essential components and KPIs that you are managing every part of every day. So I tackled them head-on and learned everything I could. Now, I can transfer those skills into the operations of my business.

Find your way. Remember, it won't be the place you end up, but you need to have a starting point, a launching point, and a frame of reference for looking back on. For example, a "my location" point to get to the "destination."

INSIDER TIP

If it were easy, everyone would do it. It WILL be hard. It WILL be a challenge. It WILL BE WORTH IT!

CHAPTER 21

THE LESSON

"Ironically, it is when we are trying to sound brilliant that we stumble, whereas when we stay within ourselves; we sound better."
—Kenny Werner

Life is most certainly full of lessons. In fact, you've experienced many of my personal and business lessons in the pages leading up to this point. Music has so many opportunities to teach lessons, and the power of it stems from how each person delivers it.

I am always working to develop myself into a better songwriter, producer, speaker, coach, and author to better deliver the power of the music. Whether I'm training at a conference for educators, social workers, psychologists, business professionals, or a group of students where I am teaching something specific about music, or I'm just sharing a song with someone who I thought might need to hear it, I am constantly learning and growing to bring even more value to those interactions.

Giving one person a musical encounter that brings an emotional response or evokes a powerful memory is what sharing that power can do for the listener—even if it's yet to be known to them at the time.

I check in weekly on the ever-changing circle of influencers, connectors, and collaborators who are continually moving in and out of my world to allow those tiny woven threads to continue stitching new ideas, new music, new skills, and new opportunities for connection.

These would be friends, family, business colleagues, clients, and new people you are meeting daily.

- Be intentional
- Share a moment
- Share a story
- Ask them for a story
- Care

More importantly, continue going back to those people regularly to check in. How are they doing? What's up next in their world? I hope t you just noticed in these last two questions that neither of them had to do with YOU. The focus was on others.

Sales-driven people use this skill and thought process daily to build their database through their sphere of influence. It's the process of planting seeds and watering them. It's harvesting those relationships over time. You don't just drop seeds in the ground on Monday and think that on Wednesday afternoon, you'll be harvesting corn to go to market.

This process can NEVER stop! The dichotomy is that it is as though you find yourself miles down this one small yet ridiculously complicated road, before the Road to 99 journey and adventure begin. Or, maybe that's when you begin to finally realize it. The thought, at last, arrives at the frontal cortex of your brain, and you have distinctive thoughts around it. You share the journey with others as you continue to grow through it.

It's hard to believe that this began as a process, leading to a journey—the meaning and purpose of living—then ultimately, it led me to the life I'm living.

While enjoying an evening of reflection and conversations around the kitchen island about the day's events with my wife, I was semi-ranting about a writing session I'd had earlier that day. Repeatedly, I hear co-writers and fellow musicians writing a song, then wanting to run and leave the process—believing they can process it in their dreams. Once again, they've taken five steps back to live in a dreamer's world. No one has ever said to stop dreaming, especially in life and in the business of music. PLEASE, keep on dreaming. But dream with a purpose.

What's the passion that makes you want to keep on showing up every day? You most certainly need to keep on showing up. Even on the hard days, because the hard days give you something else to talk and write about. They provide another opportunity to solve a puzzle and create a solution you couldn't have dreamt of before.

INSIDER TIP

**"Close some doors today.
Not because of pride, incapacity, or arrogance,
but simply because they lead you nowhere."
—Paulo Coelho**

CHAPTER 22

OUTSIDE THE BOX

"Discovery is a matter of investigation and use of imagination."
—Napoleon Hill

There are days you just want to sit in your sweatpants and binge-watch Netflix or a movie marathon. You know, you CAN sit in your sweats and write a song in between each movie or show, as well. Think outside your normal box and be creative in finding the spaces that work for you. Sometimes that leads to more opportunities and ideas for your songs or creations.

So many times, we are caught up in our mundane routines. You are creative when writing songs. You are creative in the studio. NOW, let's get creative in making more time to do more of those things. What will it take?

If you consider yourself an artist or entrepreneur, are you building a business?

A business has systems. It follows a schedule. It opens its doors for clients and creates opportunities and growth for new ones. Inside that growth is where you can begin to scale your business and manifest even more time to be creative and increase the output, collaborations, and releases.

The key is to show up! EVERY day! Not just on the days that "feel" good to you. I hear so many times from songwriters, artists, and entrepreneurs that they work when they feel good about the business. They work when there is positive and forward motion.

Wait, I thought you were running a business? This sounds like a hobby. I like to play golf and go fishing when I feel good, too, but those currently don't bring scalable revenue in the door.

Whether you're an artist, songwriter, or entrepreneur, you want to build a business, even if that business is just YOU.

"Never, Never, Never, Give Up."
—Winston Churchill

This is one of my favorite quotes, and it hangs right in front of thousands of successful people daily. For some, like me, it's part of many daily sayings, quotes, mantras, thoughts, states of mind, and so forth. It's these constant reminders that musicians, artists, CEOs, entrepreneurs, and more use to push themselves through the mundane, the obstacles, and ultimately, the points of which some might call no return.

The artist's and creator's need to live in a world of constant personal development is essential.

Reading, learning, finding mentors, and seeking to reach the next level need to be a daily focus. Though it seems this is a step so many skip in the beginning and brush it off like it is just some fluffy-head voodoo game.

READ

Start small. Begin with just ten pages each day. Stick to JUST THAT. That will allow your brain to slow down enough to be able to ingest and process what you are reading. Your brain knows it only has to singularly focus on that book for 10 minutes. As you begin down this path, you'll find that you want to push past the ten pages. When you do, make a conscious effort and be intentional about what that next step will be.

You can see by doing this that you are jumping over small hurdles and creating the habits of winners. Most people barely read one book each year. If you read only ten pages per day, and the average book is around 140-150 pages, you will average at least two books per month. Don't you think that will have an impact on your life? That means by the end of the first year of this process, you will have read at least 24 books—3360 pages—and you will have a much stronger brain.

Breaking this down makes it seem so simple. I'm a slow reader, so at first, those 10 pages took me about 20-30 minutes, depending on the font size and number of words on the page. Now I'm at about one page per minute. I've upped my game, and I do 25 minutes of personal development or mindset-driven reading and then 25 minutes of skills or technical-based reading.

GET A MENTOR

You're going to want to find mentors as well. But don't just find mentors that call themselves coaches. Make sure they are going to push you to your limits and open your mind to the possibilities you have yet to even realize. It is an investment in YOU. Don't take it lightly.

It is best if, at a minimum, you find someone who has been successful at what you are setting out to accomplish. If you are working on building your music business in the direction of songwriting and publishing, are you sure you want a coach who has never even written a song or who doesn't know what sync licensing and publishing are?

A few more things to look for with your coach:

1. Understand your strengths and weaknesses
2. You can communicate well with them
3. They are committed to making you work through the trouble spots
4. Ethics and values are similar to yours
5. You actually like them

LEARN

Then seek out where these people hang out and do business and surround yourself with these people all the time. Get in the rooms with them. Successful people seek out and find those individuals and businesses that have all seen and experienced success. Find them, get in a room with them, work with them, and LEARN as much as you can from them. Then make sure you take it one step further—bring value to them. Remember when I asked to connect with Rich in MN? It was to make HIM money through teaching lessons. Though you might not think so, you do have something of value to offer. You are you! And there is only one you. So bring your story, skills, and knowledge, and let your light shine.

If there is one thing that I have learned from working with dozens of successful musicians, entrepreneurs, and businesses, it is that they are always willing to share, help others, give advice, and at least get you started in the right direction. If you dig into their backstory far enough, you are most likely going to come across a moment when someone stuck out their "hand of knowledge" and gave them some insight that helped them surpass a few of the hurdles they may have come across on their journey.

"You don't have to be world-class at EVERYTHING
to become a successful songwriter or co-writer.
You just have to be world-class at ONE thing!

- Marty Dodson, Clay Mills, & Bill O'Hanlon,
The Songwriter's Guide to Mastering Co-Writing

When you keep putting in the time, doing the work, and showing up, you will most certainly keep on growing you and your business.

INSIDER TIP

Small actions repeated over time will get you the results you need. Keep on writing. Keep on creating. Never stop. It should be a relentless passion.

CHAPTER 23

WHERE YOUR ROAD BEGINS

"Vulnerability is the birthplace of innovation, creativity, and change."
—Brené Brown

It's an illusion
...
Making it up is my only conclusion
Staring back at
...
That's a lie. You're the only thing I'm looking at
(Song 56) -The Dumpsterfire

You've headed down the road. You've begun your journey. Or maybe you still haven't quite decided yet. That's okay, too. At this point, I hope you at least have a place to start and some tools to work with for whatever that road looks like for you.

It may be similar to the way a marathon runner begins their race. In a mob of runners standing shoulder to shoulder in the morning air, each is moving, shaking, and stretching to keep their muscles moving and engaged as the mind works its mindset magic. They breathe in the air and slowly let it out, preparing.

Your business journey begins in a mob of people trying to do similar things, reaching out to the same people. In music, it's booking the same gigs, asking the same players to play, and even trying to write with the same people.

One question you should be asking yourself is: what kind of runner or business owner do I want to be?

Have you set your distance? Notice I didn't say, "your course." It's better if you leave that up to where the road takes you. You are going to encounter curves, hills, mountains, obstacles, and more as you go.

Much like that runner, you are stepping up to the starting gate. Think about this race as a marathon, not just a 60-meter dash, or your business will be comparably over just as quick. Pick up your copy of Can't Hurt Me by Chief Navy Officer David Goggins. Read it. Digest it. Work the challenges. This will be a great start toward building the mindset you are going to need.

You need to work on those daily tasks that are going to be the rocket fuel for your mind, body, and business.

You already do these tasks daily, right?

1. Wake Up
2. Breathe
3. Blink
4. Talk
5. Stress
6. Eat

7. Relax
8. Celebrate
9. Sleep

Your new daily tasks need to be reflective of the parts of your life you want to grow, excel, and become a winner in! Find those daily tasks and work on them until they become as easy as the list above.

Here are some ideas for some daily habits to start with:

1. Write one lyrical line
2. Listen to one new song
3. Listen to one song outside your genre
4. Read 10 pages of a business or personal development book
5. Write down five things you are grateful for

This is by no means an all-inclusive list or "the" list. It's just a few brainstorms from a list that I work from daily!

You're not just trying to create new habits. Habits can be too easily broken. Look at the fitness industry; their best 10 weeks of the year take place during the last week of December and go until the first week of March.

People are trying to create new "habits" of going to the gym or working with a personal trainer. For this shift to work, there needs to be a change in mindset, which ultimately leads to a lifestyle change. It is in the change and the monotony of the mundane that we actually begin to see, feel, and experience the results.

The results start the momentum. The momentum creates forward motion. The forward motion ignites the opportunity to recycle that fuel and enhance the process as you repeat it.

Write daily.
Create daily.
Transform daily.

Don't just look for the next "cool" idea or the "hottest" new idea of the month. Study, invest, research, DO the work, and create a road for your journey to begin.

Whether your Road to 99 means:

1. 99 songs written
2. 99 recorded songs
3. 99 employees
4. 99 investment properties
5. 99 different city locations
6. $99,000 per year
7. $99,000 per month

YOU get to pick.
YOU get to run after it.
YOU get to build it.
It's YOUR Road to 99!

When that starter gun goes off for your business, what distance are you aiming for? I'm here cheering for you all the way through that extra mile 27!

I am beyond thankful for all the relationships I have already built-in business and in the music industry. The best part is that the list of amazing people is constantly growing, and I am most definitely not done on my Road to 99 because my next 99 is 99,000 sales of this book.

INSIDER TIP

Set big goals and dreams. Track them. Measure them. What gets measured gets improved.

CHAPTER 24

FAQ'S

DO I HAVE TO STAY TRUE TO ONE GENRE OF MUSIC?

I think we have already discussed this idea a bit. In co-writes, I continually suggest we write music and not get stuck or pigeonholed into a genre. Why would you want to limit any opportunity for spontaneous creation? Although sometimes you will be in a room with another writer, and they will tend to gravitate toward a specific genre, that's okay.

When Nate and I are writing, we keep the possibilities wide open, letting the song guide us. Truly, you really don't have to worry about crafting that direction until you get into production and recording. The genre will give you some direction on the types of sounds, textures, and instruments you would begin to consider. However, in the writing process, don't get too wrapped up in making all those production decisions. Write the song.

Conversely, when I'm writing with Mark, we rotate each month between something heavy metal and a dirty southern country-rock vibe—which is also great! It does give us a chance to filter out other possibilities and helps us focus on the task at hand. We both like this process, and for proof, check out Ultra-Mega and Mark Stone & The Dirty Country Band. I have included links to both of those projects on the resources page. We have been alternating releases between those two projects since March of 2020!

Both most certainly work. Just find the version that works the best for you and your co-writer, and then you'll be off to the races. There is no wrong answer or way.

Writing a song is the fine art of combining a lyric with a rhythmically interesting melody as it relates to a harmonic movement. I don't know about you, but I don't see anything in there that says it has any sort of genre attached to it.

Leave that door open. You aren't playing producer here; you are playing the role of the songwriter. That comes later. Just be patient. We've all been there.

Well, I said all that to add studying a specific genre, and the songwriters who are supplying artists with songs that are hitting the top of the charts time after time should be a journey of constant discovery and learning. Their process of continuing to write in a specific genre can give you a glimpse into their process and what "works."

I've worked extensively at listening to as many different genres of music, composers, songwriters, producers, etc., to become what Brendan called a "songwriting chameleon." I strive to be able to write, play, and produce in a style and make it feel as close to "authentic" as I can.

Breaking down what "works" can be more accurately stated as weeding out or not using the things that we already know don't work. There are hundreds and most likely thousands of repetitions and opportunities to get feedback from other artists, songwriters, producers, and ultimately the listening audiences.

One of the easiest places to start is to open your favorite streaming platform or the playlists on your iTunes account and see which songs you have played the most. Search out the songwriters for those songs. That will lead you to other songs they have written. This provides you with a feel for what they are consistently writing. You also have the opportunity to see what other genres they have ventured into.

Some writers will write songs all day long when they have publishing deals or relationships with people who are looking to cut songs. Once those are done for the day, they may choose to work on their "own" songs or collaborations for something with a completely different vibe.

If I'm working on writing on my own and flying solo, you can expect anything from country to hip-hop and rap to EDM, dance, and jazz. Check out my playlist on Spotify titled "The Inner Workings of Jeremy" and see the vast number of songs and styles I've already released.

Diving into many styles, countries, and genres of music as possible gives you a vast amount of material to pull from. Consider this the preparation for your Grammy-winning speech when you announce who your influences were and how you arrived there.

HOW MANY SONGS DO I REALLY HAVE TO WRITE?

As I've said before, it is about moving from a task that you do weekly, which will then turn into a habit and ultimately lead to a new way of thinking and living. When you approach it with this in mind, it becomes a mindset of continuing to show up.

Allow me to quote a notable Disney movie, *Finding Nemo,* with a slight twist:

"Just keep writing. Just keep writing. Just keep writing."

You're welcome for putting that little melodic hook in your brain. Earworms are powerful learning tools—ones you can also use to get you out of creative blocks. Take something that you already know, change the lyrics, and sing the same melody.

Here's a quick and very elementary example of how a few writers have done this with a song that is most likely quite familiar to you. Sing these three songs one right after one another:

1. "Twinkle, Twinkle, Little Star"
2. "ABC's"
3. "Baa, Baa, Black Sheep"

What did you notice? YES!! All of them have the same melody! In the interest of not wanting you to get in trouble with copyright infringement and thousands of dollars of legal fees, just use this as an exercise.

That said, there are opportunities for you to research public domain songs that can be reworked with new arrangements to make them your own. This happens all the time with hymns, classical music, and many common Christmas songs.

Imagine the number of songs you can add to your library by starting with some suggested melodies. I did a fun little version of "The Little Drummer Boy" with Mark Stone for Christmas of 2020. You'd think, as a drummer, I wouldn't have waited till I was 42 to finally record an arrangement of that Christmas classic.

Now, go and surround yourself with those individuals who will help you level up, the ones who want to see you succeed. These are the people who have done it before you and who have been successful. They will become your tribe, or as they call it in APEX, your syndicate. They are there to support you and cheer you on wherever you are in your journey.

Find a mentor or coach to work with. Invest in yourself. I'll tell you this right now; if you don't pay for it, you won't do it. It's called investing in yourself for a reason. There is no greater return on investment than the one in yourself.

We have more information now on how to be successful in the music business, write the best songs, release music, get music placed on TV and films, and create passive income streams in music through the biggest info tank ever. Let me spell it out for you:

G
O
O
G
L
E

AND IT'S FREE!

Yet, most people won't do it. They don't even take the time to look up what they want to know about.

But that's not who you are. You invested in this book, and that already gives you a leg up. You must invest in yourself.

Your mindset is literally the one thing that will catapult your music business into a whole other level as compared to most.

Since growing through and triumphantly completing 75 Hard, I can honestly tell you my LIFE has changed. Yes, physically, I did lose 40 pounds and feel better than I ever have in my life, but even more, I have a clarity that far surpasses that. Decisions are easier. I'm clear on where I'm headed. I might not have all the steps figured out, but I know the direction I'm headed, and I'm running full speed ahead.

Here are a few words for you to ponder for a moment.

DO
SOMETHING
DIFFERENT!

Grab a pen, and write five things next to those three words that you can do today that will make a difference.

When you grabbed that pen, you felt a moment of change, a thought, something out of the ordinary as you sat and read. Take note of that thought you had, even if for just a nanosecond, because that is the feeling you want to work toward achieving daily.

Now, it's time to sign this one, date it, and tell 10 friends about it.

Then send them over to www.Roadto99Book.com so they can grab their copy!

Sign: ____

Date: ____

Congratulations! Enjoy your journey down your own Road to 99!

ACKNOWLEDGMENTS

Though this is most certainly not an all-inclusive list, there are some people who deserve acknowledgment for their amazing support, encouragement, and nudges along the way in creating this for you.

TRACY

I'm not sure there are even enough pages for the words that would describe how amazing and supportive you are! So, I will keep it simple, "I love you, and I like you, A LOT!"

DAD

Though you've already been gone for over six years, your integrity, your lessons, your love, and watching from above were a guiding force as I put these words on these pages. Thank you for teaching me to never quit and never give up!

JEREMY WHITE

I couldn't ask for a better best friend, confidant, and amazing person in my life. Thank you for constantly pushing me to be better, want more, and soar higher than I ever thought.

THE NASHVILLE CREW

Thanks, Casey, Randy, Chad, and Travis, for letting this guy just sit in once in a while.

SAVAGE 75 HARD FACEBOOK GROUP

John Highley and the whole group were an amazing team of people who were with me through thick and thin as we triumphed over the 75 Hard program.

JEFF BREKKEN

Sir, I might even be able to say that part of this book wouldn't have come to fruition without you introducing me to the amazing network that is APEX. Thank you, brother!

NATHAN STONE

Let's face it. We ARE The Dumpsterfire! You get credit for the title of this book as you are as much a part of this journey as I am! I very much look forward to the many days to come where we can continue our days writing on the beaches of Hawaii and other amazing lands of sunshine and warmth.

ABOUT THE AUTHOR

As an interdisciplinary producer, songwriter, drummer, percussionist, speaker, author, and coach, Jeremy Schreifels has brought music to broad audiences for more than two decades. His focus across these art forms is an emotional connection, bridging lyric, rhythm, and melody to best serve the vision of both his own creations and those of the artists he works with.

Jeremy Schreifels is an avid coffee lover, dedicated father and husband, and lives and thrives with his family in the greater Minneapolis area.

In 2020 and 2021, Jeremy was involved in the writing, recording, and/or production of more than 150 songs, collaborating with musicians from around the world. Such collaborations include personnel from Toronto, the United Kingdom, the Dominican Republic, Los Angeles, and Columbia. Most notably, he has worked with Grammy-nominated mixer Brendan Ruane.

As an educator, Jeremy is an active member of the Vic Firth Education Team as a private drum teacher and marching percussion specialist. He has worked with high school marching bands, indoor drumlines, and percussion ensembles, as well as taught privately. His educational background has created further opportunities for public speaking and teaching outside the realm of percussion, including MACMH's 2018 and 2019 Annual Children's Mental Health Conferences and New Horizons Early Childhood training, among other engagements.

With a broad interest in composition, humanity, and connecting human beings through the power of song and a passion for creating, Jeremy dedicates himself to each project he's involved in, taking pride in combining orchestral finesse, an ear for modern music, building synergy in relationships, and technical studio knowledge.

MUSIC READING

The Songwriter's Guide to Mastering Co-Writing
by Marty Dodson, Clay Milles & Bill O'Hanlon

Al Schmitt on The Record, The Magic Behind the Music
by Al Schmitt with Maureen Droney

Work Hard Playlist Harder
by Mike Warner

The Artist's Journey
by Steven Pressfield

The War of Art
by Steven Pressfield

All You Need to Know About the Music Business
by Donald S. Passman

Musicophilia: Tales of Music and the Brain
by Oliver Sacks

The Stoic Drummer
by Jose Medeles

DISCLAIMER

While the author and publisher have used their best efforts in preparing this book to provide accurate information, they make no representations or warranties with respect to the accuracy or completeness of the contents.

The advice and strategies contained herein may not be suitable for your situation and are merely the opinion of the author. Consult with a professional where appropriate.

The author and publisher specifically disclaim any liability, loss, or risk, whether personal, financial, or otherwise, that is incurred as a direct or indirect consequence from the use and/or application of any contents or material of this book and/or its resources.

The purchaser and/or reader of this publication assumes all responsibility and liability for the use of these materials and information.

Adherence to all applicable laws and regulations, both advertising and all other aspects of doing business in the United States or any other jurisdiction are the sole responsibility of the purchaser and/or reader.

Made in the USA
Coppell, TX
24 March 2022